LONDON'S METRO-LAND

A unique
British railway
enterprise

Alan A Jackson

CAPITAL HISTORY

First published 2006

ISBN 185414 300 X

Published by Capital History
an imprint of Capital Transport Publishing
PO Box 250, Harrow, Middlesex

Printed by CS Graphics, Singapore

"The Metropolitan has always had one definite policy. It was that whenever the jaded Londoner went northwards in pursuit of his ideals – open air and a garden – there the Metropolitan tried to follow him." *Sir Clarendon Golding Hyde, Deputy Chairman Metropolitan Railway (1914–1933) at the opening of the Metropolitan and LNER Joint branch to Watford, 1925.*

CONTENTS

PREFACE

Metro-land is remembered by some as a 1980 novel by Julian Barnes or the 1997 film based on it. Others may recall an Evelyn Waugh character, Margot Metroland, in his *Decline & Fall* and later novels. It is also associated with Sir John Betjeman, his three 1950s poems, *Middlesex*, *Harrow on the Hill* and *The Metropolitan Railway* and his 1973 BBCtv programme *Metro-Land, a Celebration of Suburbia*. But *Metro-land*, always so punctuated (although its officials were sometimes uncertain whether its second half should begin with a capital), was current long before any of these. It emerged early in 1915 as the title of a series of annual official guides published by the Metropolitan Railway Company, and named a concept that already existed.

The term had been invented to describe the territory served by that section of the Metropolitan known as the 'Extension Line' (which ran from Baker Street to the lonely outpost of Verney Junction, 50½ miles and around two hours from central London) which offered the greatest potential for traffic development. At first, much of the area was unspoiled countryside of singular beauty and charm, only exploitable by enticing on to the railway ramblers, tourists, lovers, organisers of adult and children's outings and those pursuing the leisurely delights of fishing and golf. But already, some years before Metro-land's wartime birth in 1915, it was realised there was scope for a much more lucrative and consistently reliable addition to revenue: that ensuing from residential development of this same countryside, especially in the districts nearest to London. After World War 1, with both economic and social factors in the London region favourable to supply and demand and few effective planning constraints, this suburban and extra-urban residential expansion accelerated remarkably, continuing for a further seven years after the Metropolitan Railway Company had been swallowed up by the new London Passenger Transport Board in 1933.

Uniquely among British railway companies, the Metropolitan was able to shape a significant section of this phenomenon by exploiting its own land holdings and adding to them through the agency of subsidiary organisations and companies. Throughout, but notably from the 1910s onward, the whole process, supported by energetic publicity, was handled with great skill and dexterity by the management under R. H. Selbie. In the *Metro-land* annuals and elsewhere, the Company's copywriters spoke with breathtaking hypocrisy of the romantic beauty of the countryside served, whilst simultaneously publicising and promoting the relentless advance of uncontrolled housing development across it.

One apology is necessary. At the end of Chapter 5 is noted that almost until the end of the Metro-land era, as elsewhere, much of the speculative housebuilding in the area was the product of quite small firms. Recording this output proved tedious, as reading the result may also be for some, but after much thought, it was decided to include it in appropriate places in the main text supported by full indexing, in the hope that it will be of some value to those pursuing further research into social, local and family history. However, no claim is made that it is comprehensive.

During the preparation of my 1986 book *London's Metropolitan Railway*, I read most of the official records of the Company, a rich quarry which has also provided much of the material used here. This and the enthusiastic co-operation of David Bownes and his team at London's Transport Museum, much practical help from the publishers and generous access to their collections granted by Graham Page, Mike Miller and Trevor Wayman, have combined to make it possible to present a fully illustrated and authentic study of the Metropolitan's lengthy and energetic battle to maximise receipts from its cherished Metro-land.

ALAN A. JACKSON
Dorking, January 2006

MONEY
Money is shown in the text at contemporary price levels and can therefore only be used for comparisons in the period concerned. Conversion to current values should be made by using suitable price indices.

MEASURES
Measures are given in the contemporary form. For metric equivalents, multiply by these factors: inches to mm 25.4; feet to metres 0.3048; yards to metres 0.9144; miles to kilometres 1.6093; acres to hectares 0.4047.

ABBREVIATIONS

GCR	Great Central Railway
LMSR	London Midland & Scottish Railway
LNER	London & North Eastern Railway
LNWR	London & North Western Railway
LPTB	London Passenger Transport Board
MB	Metropolitan Borough
Met	Metropolitan Railway
Met&GCJC	Metropolitan and Great Central Joint Committee
Metro	Metropolitan Railway
MRCE	Metropolitan Railway Country Estates Ltd
SLC	Surplus Lands Committee (Met.)
UDC	Urban District Council

Official Definitions of Metro-land

'The Company has an Extension line from Baker Street that runs out into the most charming country situated in Middlesex, Herts and Bucks ... it is at this point [Wembley Park] that Metro-land really commences ... no mere print, however faithful in description, can impart the charm of the beautiful unknown country on the 'Met' so fully as a stroll through Metro-land, the rural Arcadia. Metro-land is close to London.' (*Metro-land* 1915–1916)

******

'An important Extension line from Baker Street ... runs out into the delightful country situated in Middlesex, Herts and Bucks. The district through which it passes has been happily named Metro-land, and it is the purpose of this Guide briefly to describe the more important of the small townships and villages which the Metropolitan serves, and in the steady development of which the line has been the principal agent. Metro-land is one of the most beautiful areas in the Home Counties.' (*Metro-land* 1925)

******

'METRO-LAND is a country with elastic borders which each visitor can draw for himself, as Stevenson drew his map of Treasure Island. It lies mostly in Bucks but choice fragments of Middlesex and Hertfordshire may be annexed at pleasure. As much of the countryside as you may conveniently cover afoot from one Metropolitan Railway Station to another you may add to your private and individual map of Metro-land ... Metro-land is a country of hills and valleys, ridges and bottoms, with a few broad level plateaux ... there is good tillage as well as whin-clad common, and fields which still laugh with golden corn. Here too are prim little towns which keep their old-world aspect ... Yet houses multiply and new townships rise ... This is a good parcel of English soil in which to build home and strike root ... The new settlement of Metro-land proceeds apace; the new colonists thrive amain.' (*Metro-land* 1927)

(This is an extract from an article signed only with the initial 'F'. It is notable for its closing reference to the assumed underlying purpose of Metro-land. This wording was to be repeated in each subsequent edition of *Metro-land* until the last, in 1932.)

******

1 THE TRUE EXTENT OF METRO-LAND

At first brush, Metro-land seems to defeat all attempts at establishing geographical precision. Its boundaries were constantly shifting and the 'official' definitions were not always helpful to those with tidy minds. More confusion arises because, like many a newly-born child, it existed before it had an agreed name.

Before proceeding further, it seems necessary to clarify how the term Metro-land has been interpreted for the purposes of this book, knowing that some will argue for it being used for every square yard of the Railway's catchment area between Willesden Green and Verney Junction. Whatever the pipe dreams of the managers at Baker Street offices were as they thumbed through the proofs of the latest edition of the *Metro-land* annual, we see them as hard-headed practical men, concerned primarily with maximising traffic and revenue. To them, Metro-land, despite all the pretty talk of 'rural Arcadia', 'sylvan beauty' and 'clustering old time cottages', was essentially *those parts of the area served beyond the old inner suburbs that at any given time were capable of exploitation to produce significant increases in revenue*. Primarily this meant development of new residential settlements, not just a few new houses but a serious overlay of new construction which would attract an assured and consistent return from season tickets, best of all First Class season tickets. Once this objective was achieved, the rest of the commuter's family could be expected to use the railway for London shopping and entertainment, taking the same class of travel.

To help the managers pursue this desirable objective, the Metropolitan was in a unique position regarding land ownership and purchase, as explained in the next chapter. This gave the company a considerable degree of direct control over new housing provision along the Extension line and its branches outwards from Willesden Green and even of the type of housing built. Once a Metropolitan Railway development was in place, with streets and services laid, plots could not only be sold to private individuals but in bulk to independent speculative builders conforming with the Railway's designated policy for the specific location. Individuals buying plots were offered cash advances and building plans, some from the office of the Railway's own architect. Houses were also built by the Railway's subsidiaries for direct sale with the option of purchase by regular instalments. Independent developers and builders were attracted to a district not only to participate in the Railway's own estate but by its presence were encouraged to use adjacent land in the full knowledge that they would benefit from the Railway's publicity and other assistance.

Having dismissed the idea that Metro-land extended as far as the Company's official frontier posts at Verney Junction and Brill, we are left with the problem of exactly where its outermost edges were. This is just a little easier than finding where the rainbow ends, with its legendary pot of gold. Faced with the question, the motivators and managers, people such as A. C. Ellis, R. H. Selbie, James Feiron, Henry Gibson and James Wardle would probably have answered the question in the light of the traffic and revenue situation at any given time. They too were looking for a pot of gold. Thus until around 1905, the reply would have been that the outer limit of what became known as Metro-land was Harrow-on-the-Hill, or perhaps Northwood; by the early 1920s, it would be Chorley Wood, Watford and Uxbridge, with some very exploitable gaps still lying between and later along the new Stanmore branch, also as far out as Amersham and Great Missenden. At stations beyond Great Missenden, prospects of any serious residential development were poor and London season ticket sales yielded only a low percentage of total passenger traffic receipts. It is significant that fairly consistently, the annual *Metro-land* guide had very little to say about the area north-west of Aylesbury, where opportunities for traffic development of any kind were very poor indeed (see Appendices 1 and 5 for details of receipts 'beyond Metro-land'). Right through to the last issue of *Metro-land* in 1932, nothing of much consequence was said (or advertised) regarding new residential opportunities beyond Great Missenden and at least initially there seems to have been some concern internally that the Estates Company had perhaps over-reached itself with its 1930 Weller Estate at Amersham.

A colour plate from the 1921 *Metro-land.*

AUTUMN IN METRO-LAND.

Reference to contemporary maps shows no substantial clusters of new housing appearing around or near any of the stations between Amersham and Aylesbury, apart from a small amount of growth at Wendover north westwards, parallel with the railway. A table produced by the Metropolitan Railway's Audit Office at the end of 1928 gives the number of season tickets issued for travel over the Metropolitan Railway in 1921 compared with the number issued eight years later at these stations, expressed as the equivalent of monthly tickets. Serious commuters were most plentiful at Great Missenden, where the figures were 874 and 1,289 but numbers then faded away steeply: at Wendover, 280 and 324; at Stoke Mandeville, a mere 32 and 62; and at Aylesbury only 423 in 1921 and three fewer in 1928. By 1933 all that could be said about new housing construction beyond Great Missenden, in a paper prepared for an official inspection by LPTB and LNER officials, was that at Wendover 'some houses' were available near the station and plots were also available.

Looking through the publicity relevant to the stations between Amersham and Aylesbury (inclusive), we can see that some importance was attached to the development of what might be described as pleasure traffic. Throughout the 1910s, 1920s and even in the 1930s, car ownership amongst the Greater London middle classes was quite thinly distributed and where cars were owned, their use was far less intensive than it is today. Only a very tiny proportion of those in the lower salary ranges could afford both a mortgage and a motor car, a fact sometimes overlooked by modern social historians. The relative expense of air and long distance rail/sea travel meant that those able to finance an annual holiday of a week or two mostly went to a British resort; shorter breaks, weekends and other outdoor leisure time would be spent in the countryside close to London, the majority using public transport. This contributed to the success of the efforts made from the 1900s onwards by the Metropolitan and its Great Central Railway partner in the Joint Line to attract walkers and short break holidaymakers into the high Chilterns north west of Amersham, but the additional contribution to revenue this made was not particularly significant. In 1920–22, at the request of the Minister of Transport, some excursions were run from Aldgate or Liverpool Street to Aylesbury and the number of tickets sold was reported by John Wardle (Commercial Manager) to R. H. Selbie (General Manager). Details of the results (see Appendix 4) indicate the fickle nature of this traffic and show no strong preference by excursionists for stations beyond Amersham.

Even as late as the early 1930s, the area beyond Great Missenden showed little evidence of qualifying as authentic Metro-land. There is no indication in the surviving Board minutes and reports that its pleasure traffic was regarded as particularly valuable in revenue terms or consistently strong, or that it was being exploited or considered exploitable for any significant residential construction, this last despite the lack of any effective planning legislation in the between-war years. As a residential area for London-based commuters, even those with above average incomes, the type of train service the Metropolitan was able to provide at these outer stations involved a journey too tedious to be tolerated daily by those working in the business and administration centres of the City and Westminster. In 1933, the times to reach Baker Street were 46–66 minutes from Great Missenden, 54–74 minutes from Wendover, 59–79 minutes from Stoke Mandeville and 49–85 minutes from Aylesbury.

For all these reasons, it can be argued that until its last days, Metro-land proper had been well and truly left behind once a Down train had pulled away from Great Missenden, a point no more than halfway to the official outposts of the Metropolitan Railway.

Nevertheless, despite its somewhat unproductive character in revenue terms, which in our view excludes it from detailed consideration as genuine Metro-land, the section beyond Great Missenden was not without its moments, of which some account is given in Appendix 4.

From the early 1900s until its demise, the Metropolitan kept up the effort to attract what it called 'pleasure traffic', as evidenced by this 40-page 1929 'New Edition' of *Country Walks*, issued jointly with the LNER.

2 COLONISING AND PUBLICISING THE EXTENSION LINE 1880–1914

When the Metropolitan Railway was preparing to build its Extension line north west from Swiss Cottage to Harrow in the the mid-1870s, it acquired a considerable addition to its already significant property holdings. Large parcels of grassland totalling some 400 acres either side of the new railway between Willesden Green and Kingsbury were purchased from the Ecclesiastical Commissioners and two other landowners, John & Catherine Prout and Finch. The board accepted that it was 'more economical and desirable' to buy in this quantity than obtain it piecemeal, under notice. At this time the only motivation behind driving the Extension line north westwards beyond built-up London was Chairman Sir Edward Watkin's desire somehow to link the Metropolitan Railway with railways in the Midlands. However it was not long before uses would be found for surplus lands.

SIR EDWARD WATKIN, BART., M.P

In 1880–81 it was decided to use part of the land immediately east of the River Brent between what are now Neasden and Wembley Park stations for new rolling stock and locomotive facilities. As the area was still quite rural, 112 cottages and houses and and ten shops with living space over were completed in 1882 for the incoming Neasden employees. To house the additional staff required for the new electric power station, the estate was enlarged in 1904–05 by adding 44 houses, with some of the shops converted to residential accommodation.

The development of further areas of the remaining surplus land was also begun at this time, with an independent solicitor granting building leases and introducing builders on the 12-acre Willesden Park Estate, south of the railway and close to the new Willesden Green station. During 1880–81, sewered roads were laid out and trees planted along them, all at the Railway Company's expense and the first building leases were granted for semi-detached villas in October of the latter year, with the houses coming into occupation in 1881–83. The Metropolitan's Land Committee's report for the second half of 1881 noted '. . . there is little doubt that the estate will be a residential property providing a considerable income and aiding in the development of traffic'. This was the precursor of some 50 years of active involvement in the supply of residential accommodation to provide traffic in the catchment area of the Extension line and its branches.

It should be said at this point that by the mid 1880s, Sir Edward Watkin, the Metropolitan's chairman, had become nervous of parliamentary opposition to a small railway company continuing to hold on to and develop a substantial estate surplus to railway purposes, despite various special provisions included in the Metropolitan's private acts up to this time. In the Land Clauses Act of 1845, Parliament had enshrined a principle that a railway company should sell off all land not required for the purposes of the railway's special Acts within a maximum of ten years from the expiry of the time limited by the special Acts for the completion of the works. It continued to be regarded as public policy that a railway company should not hold on to land not required for railway purposes beyond this time limit unless this was specifically authorised by Parliament. Steps were therefore taken to divide the Company's Ordinary Stock into two parts, treating the surplus lands and the railway revenue separately. This was authorised by an Act of 1885 and after the required approval by 75 per cent of the shareholders, the proposal received final Parliamentary blessing by the scheduling of the scheme to the Metropolitan's Act of 1887. Although the surplus property all remained very firmly vested in the Railway Company, its management now passed to a new Surplus Lands Committee (SLC) which maintained accounts for the surplus estate income from rents, etc. and the proceeds of sales, this to be applied to the payment of dividends on the Surplus Lands stock. The SLC could and did receive loans from the Railway Company for further land purchases and payment of dividends.

Finally, in this raft of legislation, the Metropolitan Railway Act, 1898 allowed the Surplus Lands Committee to improve, develop and lay out for building any of its lands, including those acquired 'hereafter'. The Committee was also authorised to purchase and retain leasehold lands, erect houses and buildings and carry out structural alterations and improvements.

Station Road and Walm Lane, Willesden Green, c 1905, viewed from the Metropolitan Railway station. South of the station, the Willesden Park Estate was developed by the Railway between 1880 and 1883.

Meanwhile, back at Willesden Green, more building leases were granted, including some on additional land in Walm Lane, purchased by the railway to complete the Willesden Park Estate. A second section, further west, between Villiers Road and the railway was laid out in the 1890s. As the 19th century drew to a close, some 350 houses had been erected here and Willesden Council was asking for a station to serve what was rapidly becoming a new suburb. This facility was not immediately granted but with some 3,000 houses built or building in the neighbourhood and around 10,000 people living south of the railway between Willesden Green and Neasden in 1904 and the population still growing, the pressure became irresistible. A new island platform station named Dollis Hill and Gladstone Park was finally provided from 1 October 1909. After five months, with a second entrance from Chapter Road available from 10 December 1909 and with allowance made for traffic transferring from the stations either side, it was calculated there had been an approximate 50 per cent return on construction costs.

There was also some activity further down the line at Harrow. In 1888, the SLC put building plots in Pinner Road and College Road to auction, achieving modest success.

Development of two SLC estates was well under way before 1914. At Cecil Park, south of the railway at Pinner, some houses were completed and occupied by 1901 and advertisements for them were exhibited on stations free of charge. This estate included some very large three-storey semis, with three reception rooms and up to six bedrooms. Leases here were up to £70 a year, compared with an average of £50 at Willesden Park. Further building leases were granted in 1911–12, also at the adjacent Stanley Villas (named after Stanley Eyles, the SLC surveyor). Around 1913, Cecil Park residents gained an entrance to the Down side of Pinner station. Also at Pinner, the Grange Estate, on the Up side of the line, was begun by the SLC just before World War 1 but did not really get under way until the 1920s.

In about 1905 a proud mother with her baby and nurse pose at the north end of Cannon Lane in front of contemporary middle class railway-related housing, a short walk south of Pinner station.

Wembley Park Drive in the 1920s with the first housing on the Wembley Park Estate visible through the trees.

Wembley Park 1890–1915: Changing roles

At beginning of 1890, the Railway Company and the SLC purchased the 280-acre Wembley Park Estate on the south side of the line between Neasden and Harrow, just over six miles from Baker Street. This move was a response to an initiative generated by Sir Edward Watkin, the Railway's chairman, who had been seized with the idea of building a taller and larger version of the Eiffel Tower which would stand as the visible symbol of London's finest sports, leisure and exhibition centre, served by the Metropolitan Railway. A 1,150ft tower was to be erected at the south end of a 124-acre Tower Park (as we shall call it to distinguish this area from the rest of the Wembley Park Estate), and a separate Tower Company had been formed on 14 August 1889 to bring Watkin's concept to realisation. This Company, with initial capital subscribed by Metropolitan Railway shareholders (Watkin had the largest holding) acquired the whole of the Wembley Park Estate on mortgage from 24 November 1898, the intention being that the remainder of the area should be set aside eventually to accommodate commuter housing so that the whole would generate a very considerable new traffic for the Extension line.

The Tower Park, with its 8-acre boating lake fed by the River Brent, variety hall, cricket ground, running and trotting track, tea house, two restaurants, band stand and Watkin's partly-built Tower at its south end, was opened to the public as a pleasure resort on 12 May 1894, together with the adjacent station (which had been used for occasional football traffic since the previous October). A long siding had been laid into the park for construction of the Tower and other features. A total of 120,000 people were attracted for the first full season in 1895. Roads were also built into the western section of the estate at this time, these later to be named Wembley Park Drive, Oakington Avenue and Raglan Gardens.

However, despite a substantial injection of funds by the owners, both the public and investors showed little interest in Watkin's project. Although lifts were provided, most of those coming into the Park after public access was allowed to the Tower's 155ft high first platform in 1896 did not bother to go up. The separate company formed for its construction went into voluntary liquidation in 1899. After the 1902 season, the partly-built structure, its foundations tilting in the treacherous Middlesex clay, was declared unsafe. Demolition followed in 1906–07, making use of the siding installed for its erection and its site was left fallow until it was occupied by the 1923 Stadium.

With the unsuccessful Tower Company not having paid its mortgage liability for 4½ years, the Metropolitan Railway board decided in 1905 to develop most of the land as a residential estate 'in the interests of the railway company'. The Tower Company, which had already tested the water by erecting two houses in Wembley Park Drive in 1899–1900, emerged in new guise in October 1906 as The Wembley Park Estate Company Ltd, the Railway's control continuing after filling its Board with Metropolitan directors. From 1906, agreements were made with J. H. Comben and later, other builders, to construct drains and roads and erect houses; plots were sold off at £650–£750 an acre. Two years later, a hundred house plots were auctioned on the site. After some brief temporary uses (the Variety Hall was used as film studios by the Walturdaw Co. from 1907 until its wooden structure was largely destroyed by fire in January 1911), the southern part of the Tower Park was let to the Wembley Park Golf Company at £600 p.a., becoming a 9-hole course, enlarged to 18 holes in 1912. The future of the Tower Park then remained undecided until 1922, when its land, with some adjacent open areas, 216 acres in all, was sold to the British Empire Exhibition Assets Company Ltd to serve as the site of the 1924/1925 Exhibition. The proceeds from this deal enabled the Wembley Park Estate Company to discharge the 1898 mortgage, providing a welcome boost to the Railway Company's finances.

An artist's impression of the proposed Wembley Park, boating lake and Tower seen from the station.

Wembley Park, boating lake and partially-completed Tower (on the present Stadium site) as it appeared c 1905.

In the early 1910s houses were built on the west side of the Estate in Wembley Park Drive, Oakington Avenue and Raglan Gardens (renamed Empire Way in 1924). The Railway Company offered loans at 4 per cent from its Reserve Fund to finance 'builders of good standing' and in 1913 money from the Fund was made available to assist direct building by the Estate Company. By early 1915, the residential area of Wembley Park contained 106 houses, most in a more modern style than those at Willesden Park or Cecil Park. Although the Estate Company had not managed to pay any dividend, its activities had pushed up receipts at Wembley Park station from £3,807 in 1906 to £6,150 in 1914 but, with the onset of World War 1, demand for houses fell sharply. To alleviate the Estate Company's situation and encourage its efforts at development, it was then agreed that for seven years the Railway Company would make it an annual allowance equivalent to 25 per cent of the increase in receipts from such traffic at Wembley Park station as was over and above the receipts there for 1906, subject to a maximum of £700 a year. Further details of the development of the Wembley Park Estate are given in Chapter 3 and Appendix 2.

Rickmansworth High Street looking west c 1914. At the extreme left, the 1912 Electric Picture Playhouse (cinema) in the converted old Town Hall.

Independent housebuilding and traffic development 1880–1914

With the opening of the Extension line from Willesden Green to Harrow-on-the-Hill on 2 August 1880, the area served was described in an official guide which appears to be the first of a long line of publications related to what would later be known as Metro-land. It was followed by the clumsily-titled *The Metropolitan Railway Extension to Harrow and Pinner, Northwood, Rickmansworth, Chenies and Chesham* written by Luke Ellis, an updated version of the 1880 booklet. Publication was contemporary with the opening of the railway from Rickmansworth to Chesham on 8 July 1889.

There is an isolated advertisement in the 1889 booklet (p.17) of considerable interest to our theme. This shows that one local landowner was a step ahead of the Metropolitan in quickly grasping the likelihood of property values appreciating following the provision of railway services allowing convenient (at least half-hourly) and reasonably fast access to central London. The announcement concerned the '800-acre Eastbury Estate' at Northwood, described as having 40ft wide roads recently constructed with water mains being laid and it offered plots of one half to ten acres for sale or lease for building houses.

This estate, which covered much of the area east of the railway within walking distance of the station, had been purchased by the multi-named Frank Murray Maxwell Hallowell Carew (1866–1943) in March 1887, less than six months before the opening of the line though Northwood. Between September that year and July 1891, ten

Advertisements.

NORTHWOOD,

ON THE BORDERS OF HERTS AND MIDDLESEX.

Unquestionably one of the most Picturesque and Healthy Districts within easy reach of Town.

THE EASTBURY ESTATE,

Which has only recently been rendered accessible by rail through the enterprise of the Metropolitan Railway Company in extending their line to Rickmansworth, occupies a most important position in this delightfully rural part of the country.

The entirety of the Estate comprises about 800 acres,
the whole of which is beautifully undulating and luxuriantly timbered Pasture Land. It possesses all the essential features for

RESIDENTIAL PURPOSES,

sloping gradually to the South, and being at the same time sheltered from the North by extensive Woodlands, forming part of the property.

It is well situated for access, being only 35 minutes' ride by rail from London, and is served by a half-hourly service of trains, the Northwood station being centrally placed upon the property.

The air is of a particularly healthy and bracing character, and the WATER SUPPLY IS UNDOUBTEDLY OF THE PUREST, the mains of the Colne Valley Water Company being laid on to the Estate. **Excellent Roads** of a width of 40 feet have been constructed and

THE FREEHOLD OF THE FRONTAGES
thus created is now
TO BE SOLD OR LET ON BUILDING LEASES
IN AREAS VARYING FROM HALF AN ACRE TO TEN ACRES,
according to position, and
TO SUIT THE REQUIREMENTS OF PURCHASERS.

FOR PARTICULARS APPLY TO

MESSRS. HUMBERT, SON & FLINT,
Land Agents & Surveyors,
Lincoln's Inn Fields, London, W.C., & Watford, Herts.

b

Within two years of the Metropolitan's arrival in Northwood, a private landowner seizes the opportunity to exploit the enhanced value of his domain (advertisement in the Railway's guide of 1889).

Opposite Northwood, Moor Park and Rickmansworth, a shown on the Watford & District footpaths map of 1914.

auctions were held for freehold building lots in unmade roads mostly bearing Carew's five names and those of other members of his family, including his second wife's stage name. Carew, who did not build a single house here himself, allocated sites for shops in Green Lane, Maxwell Road and High Street and arranged protective covenants to ban industrial development anywhere on the estate. He also ensured social class separation by requiring purchasers to build the more expensive houses in Carew and Maxwell and Dene Roads, a species of second class in Chester and Murray Roads and low value terraced cottage property on the west side of the High Street. By 1901 Northwood, where the census found but 409 well-scattered inhabitants in 1881, had a neatly-zoned population of 2,500 in 496 houses, many in the urban streets near the railway.

Around Harrow-on-the-Hill station, following the SLC auction already mentioned and other land sales, the first two decades of the 20th century saw considerable new residential development in Greenhill, north of the line. Here, the Headstone, Greenhill Park, Marlborough Hill, Elm Grove, Roxborough Close and Belmont Park estates were all within half to three quarters of a mile of the Metropolitan station. On the Headstone Estate alone, four auctions, involving 282 plots for medium-size villas were held between July 1899 and June 1901, each offering a free luncheon and free conveyance from the station.

Similarly convenient of access to the trains were the houses on the New Bessborough Estate and along other roads south of the Extension line and the first quarter mile of the Uxbridge branch. This development stimulated the opening on 17 November 1913 of West Harrow, a crudely-built halt with two 350ft timber platforms. Within two years, this facility was attracting around 43,000 passengers a month, with no erosion of business at the main Harrow station.

Much of 'Metropolitan' Harrow took the form of gabled bay-windowed terraces offering three or four bedrooms and two reception rooms. Contemporary prices ranged from £230–£480 and by 1906 some were being offered with electric wiring.

Further out, at Pinner, things were also beginning to stir. By 1910 Ronald S. Townly (of Westcliff on Sea) had plots for sale on his 19-acre estate, with frontages to Paines Lane and Waxwell Lane (described as 'charming and picturesque old parish roads') and to the main London–Northwood Road. Here houses were being erected 'under the direct supervision of a well-known London architect' (though not apparently sufficiently famous for his name to be mentioned). A particular feature of Pinner, both at this time and after World War 1, was the large number of small building firms involved, often more than one in the same road; those in search of further detail are recommended to consult Elizabeth Cooper's careful study, noted in the Select Bibliography.

Northwood was at this time the outer limit of significant new residential development along the line. Its superior housing, in the form of detached villas on quite large plots, was to be found east and west of the railway, mostly north of the station but within easy reach of it. The sale of the extensive Eastbury Estate was now bearing fruit. Quality houses were to be found in Frithwood Avenue, Eastbury Avenue, Carew Road and Watford Road. These were supplemented on the west side of the line by others of similar value as far west as the Rickmansworth Road. Harry Neal arrived at Northwood in 1907, quickly establishing a business which erected more such houses, some with as many as six bedrooms. In 1913 Neal bought the Oxhey Woods Estate and, as we shall see, his company was very active in the area between the wars.

Pinner, as shown on Watford & District footpaths map of 1914.

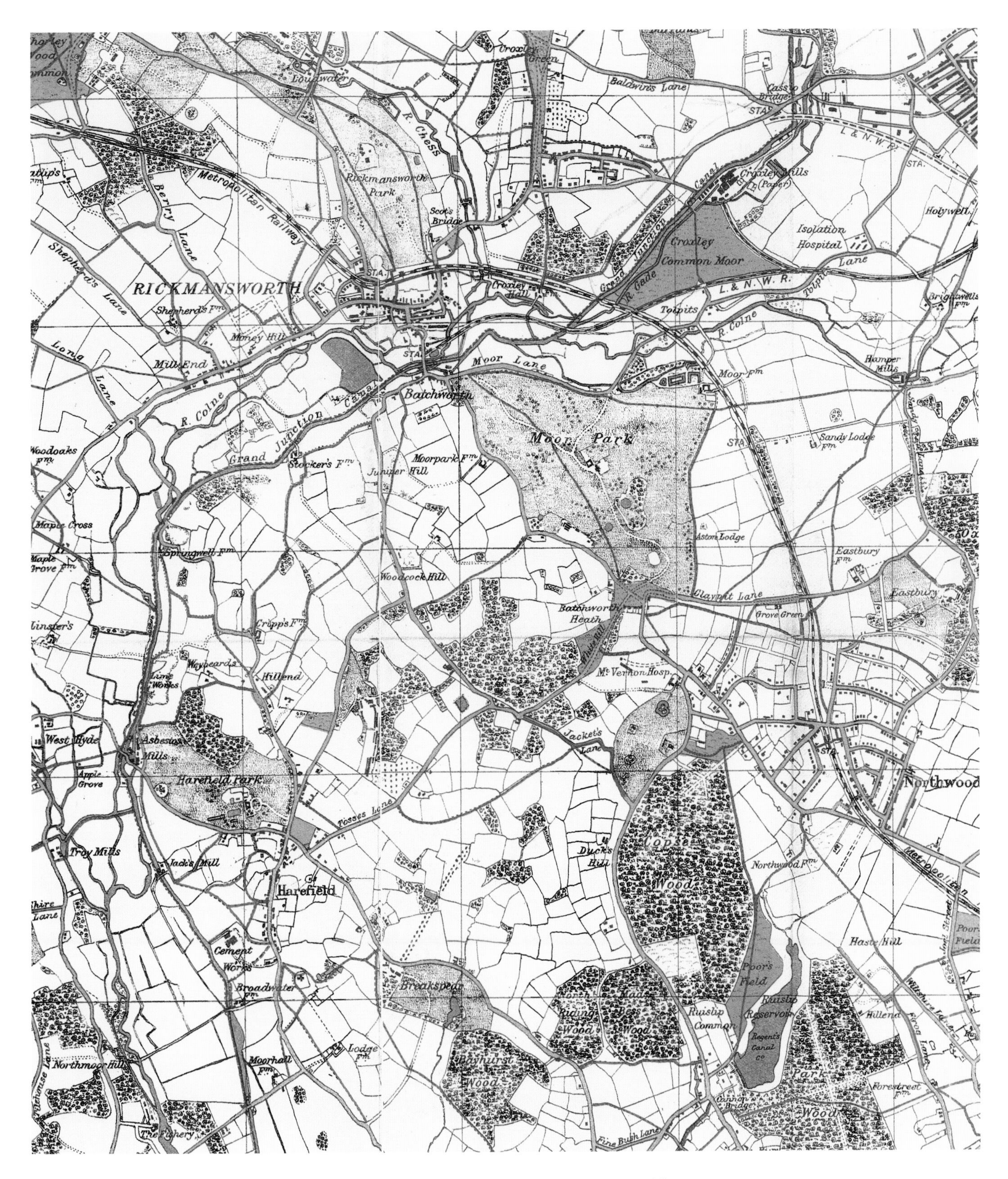
RICKMANSWORTH
Rickmansworth Park
Scot's Bridge
R. Chess
Loudwater
Croxley Green
Baldwin's Lane
Cassio Bridge
STA.
L. & N. W. R.
Croxley Mills (Paper)
Holywell
Isolation Hospital
Croxley Common Moor
R. Gade
Grand Junction Canal
Metropolitan Railway
Berry Lane
Shepherd's Lane
Shepherd's Fm
Croxley Hall Fm
Tolpits
Tolpits Lane
R. Colne
Brightwells Fm
Money Hill
Mill End
Long Lane
Moor Lane
Moor Fm
Hamper Mills
Batchworth
Moor Park
Sandy Lodge Fm
Woodoaks Fm
Grand Junction Canal
Stocker's Fm
Juniper Hill
Moorpark Fm
Aston Lodge
Maple Cross
Maple Grove Fm
Springwell Fm
Eastbury Fm
Eastbury
Woodcock Hill
Batchworth Heath
Glaypit Lane
Grove Green
Cripps's Fm
Waybeards
Lime Works
Hillend
Mt. Vernon Hosp.
Jacket's Lane
West Hyde
Asbestos Mills
Apple Grove
Harefield Park
Tosses Lane
Northwood
Troy Mills
Jack's Mill
Duck's Hill
Copse Wood
Northwood Fm
Harefield
Metropolitan
Cement Works
Broadwater Fm
Breakspear
Haste Hill
Poor's Field
North Riding Wood
Mad Bess Wood
Ruislip Common
Ruislip Reservoir
Regent's Canal Co
Hillend
Lodge Fm
Northmoor Hill
Moorhall Fm
Mayhurst Wood
Park Wood
Forestreet Fm
Cannon Bridge
The Fishery
Fine Bush Lane

Ruislip station looking east c 1908.

Ruislip: Town planning but Garden Suburb schemes frustrated

South of Northwood, on the Harrow–Uxbridge branch (opened in 1904, electrified in 1905) railway-influenced Edwardian residential development was almost entirely confined to two sites. Some medium-sized detached houses were spattered over the area bounded by Sharp's Lane, Wood Lane and the road from the station to Ruislip village. The greater part of this was in the Ruislip Park House Estate, which had been laid out around 1906 with new streets called Manor Road, King Edward Road and Church Avenue, the houses following slowly some years later. Others appeared from 1907 in King's End Avenue, which from 1905 afforded a direct link between Kingsend Farm and the railway station.

To introduce the second area, mention must be made of the new (1904) Ruislip-Northwood UDC's pioneer use of Britain's very first Town Planning legislation. An enabling Act of 1909, introduced by an idealistic Liberal Government, allowed local councils to draw up schemes which could impose specific requirements relating to new building developments, subject to general approval by a new central government body, the Local Government Board. Ruislip's scheme, drawn up in conjunction with King's College, Cambridge, a major landowner in this district, covered 5,750 acres and set out out distances between building lines; building design requirements; control of outdoor advertising; the location of shopping and industrial areas and, most importantly, graduated zones of permitted densities of housing. The average density of housing was to be highest (12 to the acre) south of the Metropolitan Railway and in the extreme west near Ruislip & Ickenham station (Great Western & Great Central Railway Joint). In the centre of the district it was reduced almost entirely to eight, but in the north west around the Reservoir and further north, only an average of four to the acre were to be allowed. Such social zoning assumed considerable significance, since well over two thirds of the planning area was allocated to housing, leaving only 234 acres for industry in the low lying land alongside the GW&GCJt in the extreme south of the district.

Alongside the town planning scheme, King's College was anxious to promote 'garden city' type development on its land in the centre of the council's area. A new company, Ruislip Manor Ltd, was formed in 1910 to lay out and develop the whole 1,300 acres of the College's estate in the area on garden city lines, over a period of 21 years. On 2 October 1911, a second body, the Ruislip Manor Cottage Society Ltd, was incorporated for the purpose of taking up College land and building, letting or selling 'small houses and cottages,' chiefly on the site known as Manor Farm, north of the Metropolitan Railway as far as Eastcote Road and east of the road between Ruislip station and the village. In an early step towards this, the Cottage Society obtained the agreement of the Metropolitan Railway to build Ruislip Manor Halt, between Ruislip and Eastcote stations. This was duly opened on 5 August 1912 without any road access; on its north side there was a footpath leading back to Ruislip station and another into Manor Way and Windmill Way, the lonely, very tentative beginnings of the Cottage Society's proposed architect-designed development. The first 'cottages' were erected at the corner of Manor Way and the Eastcote Road, then 12 along Manor Way in 1911–12, followed by a further 14 in Windmill Way during 1913–14. All work then ceased following the outbreak of World War 1, when the light railway and tip wagons used to bring building materials up from the Metropolitan Railway's freight yard at Ruislip station became playthings for local youth. After the war there was some minimal resumption of activity but most of the site was sold to independent developers.

Ruislip Manor: two houses at the junction of Manor Way (right). Designed by Michael Bunney and Clifford C Makins AARIBA and erected for Ruislip Manor Cottage Society Ltd in 1912. Still extant in 2006, their external walls have grey and brown Tring bricks below soft red hanging tiles and the dark red roof tiles are hand-made. The half timber work is of oak and the plaster filling is left with a smooth trowelled face. The accommodation was originally described as 'living room, parlour, kitchen, three bedrooms, bathroom and two WCs'. The 1912 rent was 16s a week.

General Plan of Manor Farm Area (130 acres) round Windmill Hill, between Ruislip Manor Halt (Metropolitan Railway) and Ruislip Village.

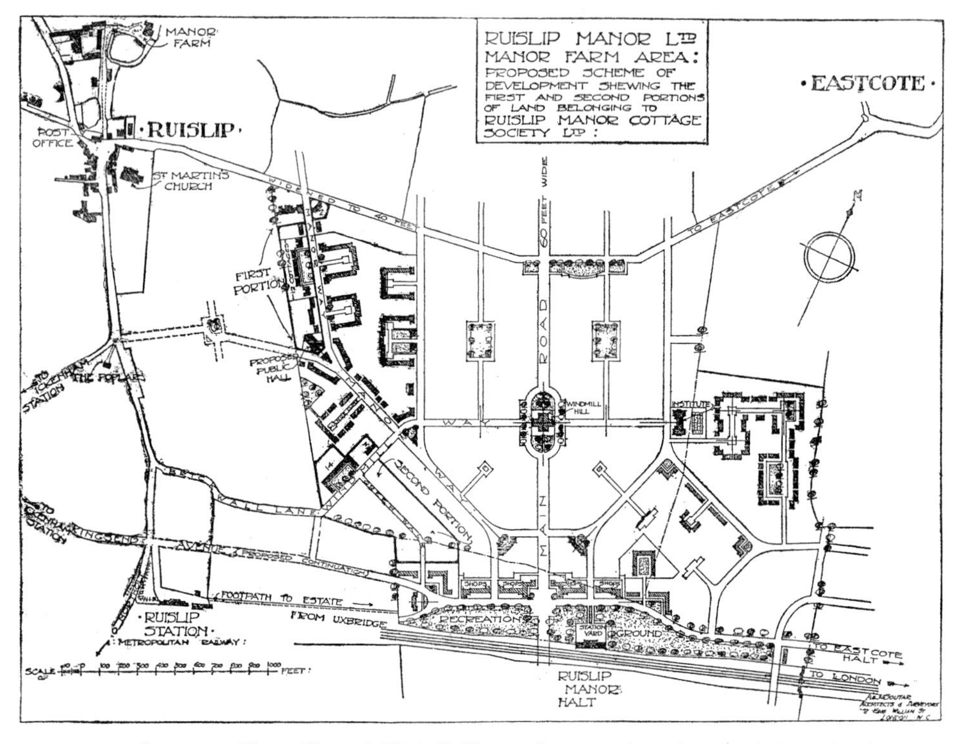

Facing **Ruislip Manor Halt,** which the Railway Company have agreed to make forthwith, and the adjacent Recreation Grounds, a fine shopping centre will be formed, from which new roads will lead west to Kingsend Estate, east to Eastcote, north-west by Manor Way to Ruislip Schools and Church, and north by a main road 60 feet wide to the Eastcote Road, Northwood and London. **A footpath** will run parallel with the railway to the present Ruislip Station, and a new road will run to Ickenham Station from Manor Way.

The Cottage Society have taken up a gross area of 10 acres, and have commenced building 14 houses on the sites marked **"First Portion,"** near the Schools, Manor Way. Contracts are being obtained for 17 houses on the site marked "Second Portion," fronting on Windmill Way.

The lay-out shows houses grouped about greens and in quadrangles or closes, so as to preserve the existing amenities, and to give residents that restfulness and quiet so much desired by those who spend their days in the busy city.

Cottages will also be erected along the Green Walk and adjoining closes, shown in detail on the plan of the **Second Portion,** which appears on another page. Manor Way and Windmill Way are in course of completion, and the road-making operations show that **the sub-soil of the Cottage Society's land consists of a deep stratum of sand,** much of which is silver sand. The surface soil is excellent for gardening operations.

Sites for proposed Institutes, Churches and additional open spaces are shown on the plan.

7

Map of the Ruislip Manor Cottage Society's Manor Farm Estate. Ruislip, from the company's 1912 brochure.

As yet there remained a great expanse of unspoilt Middlesex countryside between Ruislip Manor and West Harrow, with a single isolated foretaste of what was yet to come, one that had helped to prompt the Ruislip-Northwood UDC and King's College to consider a town planning scheme and also one that had been encouraged by the proximity of the Metropolitan Railway's electric train service. South of Eastcote village in 1909, the British Freehold Investment Syndicate had begun to sell plots of 100ft by 20ft along grids of unsurfaced streets either side of the railway adjacent to the halt which had been opened on 26 May 1906 to serve Eastcote. North of the railway, the soft-topped roads had received archetypical suburban names: Acacia Avenue, Myrtle Avenue, Hawthorne Avenue, Elm Avenue and Lime Grove. The Syndicate's sole objective was to maximise its profits – it had no idealistic inclination to guide and regulate what was erected on the land sold. Some of the purchasers appear to have put up shanty type bungalows on their plots but although hundreds of plots were sold, in 1913 the men from the Ordnance Survey found only two or three permanent houses and the first advertisement for such houses (by Lime Grove Freeholds Ltd) did not appear in the London *Evening News* until 8 October that year.

In Eastcote, mains water, sewers and refuse disposal were all available by 1914, not to mention the frequent electric trains to and from central London, but in the Eastcote area as a whole, only 125 plans for new housing had been passed in the years 1909–14 (including some for the Ruislip Manor Cottage Society) and not all of these may have been completed before wartime exigencies stopped further construction. For the time being, a more important element in the traffic at Eastcote Halt was that generated by inner London pleasure seekers, notably children's outings. These last came in noisy crowds to enjoy the countryside and in particular the delights of the Pavilion Gardens, a 16-acre site on the west side of Field End Road south of the railway, owned and managed by a Salvation Army Bandmaster, Albert E. Bayly. Selbie reported to the Board on 12 March 1914 that in July 1913, 93 parties, 16,000 passengers in total, had arrived: sometimes at the rate of 3,000 a day. There was some concern about accidents; it was agreed the platforms be widened from 8ft 4in to 12ft and various other improvements be made. Amongst those patronising Eastcote's delights in the summer were the children of the employees at Neasden, carried free in special trains.

At the time of the opening of the Metropolitan's Uxbridge branch (July 1904), a journalist had remarked that many of the local landowners were said to be averse to allocating land for house building, this suggesting that the hope of establishing a large population along the new line did not promise early realisation. And so it was to be for some years, partly due to the fact that there were still many areas closer to London where new houses were available at reasonable prices (and lower fare cost) but also to the interruption of the four years of World War 1 and the social and economic upheaval that followed. But the relative inactivity that gave this part of Metro-land another decade or so of rural peace was not for want of publicity sponsored by the Metropolitan Railway.

Wooden platforms with paraffin lamps and not a house in sight – Eastcote Halt c 1920.

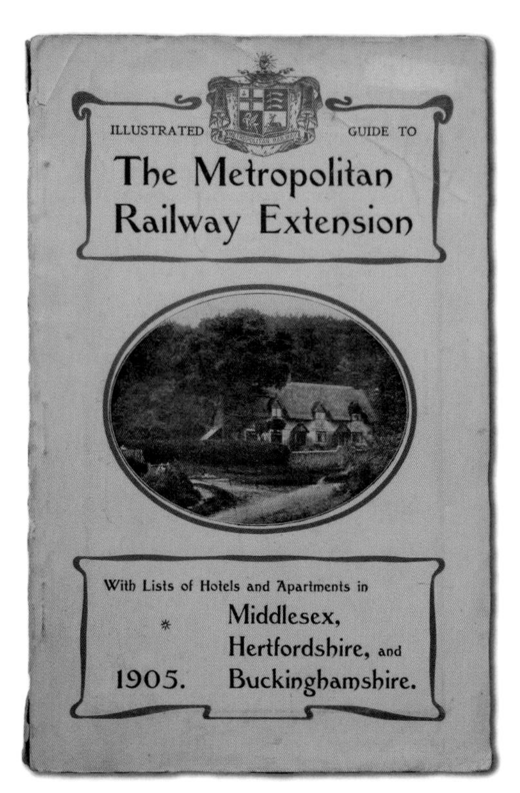

Cover of the 1905 guide to the Metropolitan Railway's country areas, mainly concerned with pleasure traffic.

The importance of publicity realised 1903–14

Printing techniques allowing reproduction of acceptable colour images and black & white photographs had advanced significantly, becoming much cheaper by the turn of the century. In the 1900s and early 1910s this encouraged the railway companies, including the Metropolitan, to pay more attention to publicity as a means of building up and sustaining higher levels of traffic.

The Railway Magazine of June 1903 reviewed 'a neat and unpretentious little guide' issued by the Metropolitan with a text that explained the route of the Extension line and gave short descriptions of the district surrounding each station. The magazine remarked that 'Mr Ellis [General Manager of the Metropolitan 1901–08] certainly seems alive to the possibilities of the hitherto little-exploited country which his line reaches'. Indeed the new guide proved something of a milestone, establishing a pattern which was to continue without much substantial alteration (but with significant additions) over the following 30 years.

In 1904 a twopenny brochure with a coloured cover was produced for the opening of the new line between Harrow and Uxbridge in July that year. Again the plan was to describe and illustrate the areas on a station by station basis. The *Illustrated Guide to the Metropolitan Railway Extension* appeared again in 1904 and 1905, with the same emphasis on using the railway as a means of enjoying the attractive countryside it served between Wembley Park and Wendover and along the Uxbridge line. There was but the briefest of mentions of the Metropolitan's extremities beyond Aylesbury.

As much of the appealing country areas along the Extension line were jointly served by the Metropolitan and Great Central Railway companies, it was no surprise when in March 1906 the Metropolitan Board was informed by Ellis that an annual guide to the Extension line was now to be produced with the GCR, who had agreed to pay half the cost; 20,000 copies had been ordered, with a revised text and new photographs.

By now Ellis was becoming concerned at the slow build-up of traffic on the still almost entirely rural Harrow and Uxbridge line. In May 1907 the Board approved his proposal for a booklet to advertise the attractions of the district served, with emphasis on its suitability for residential purposes and for excursion, weekend and holiday traffic. Ten thousand copies were ordered at a cost of around £120 but to reduce the net outlay, advertisements were included and Ellis supplied the photographs from his own camera. This publication duly appeared in 1908, along with the annual guide to the Metropolitan & GCR Joint line.

Also in that year, an opportunity was seized to gain a small increase in Extension revenue by providing two timber side-platforms and a small ticket office at Preston Road, initially to serve the 37-acre grounds of the Uxendon Shooting Club, host to clay pigeon shooting events during the 1908 London Olympic Games. A guaranteed income of £200 a year had been offered and trains stopped here on request from 21 May 1908. Further business was obtained when the Harrow Golf Club opened its club house and 18-hole course just south of the railway and west of Preston Road in 1912 and in the period 1910–14, the nucleus of a new residential community appeared along the road to the hamlet of Preston north of the halt. As we shall see, the area on both sides of the line was destined to see vigorous residential development in the late 1920s and the 1930s.

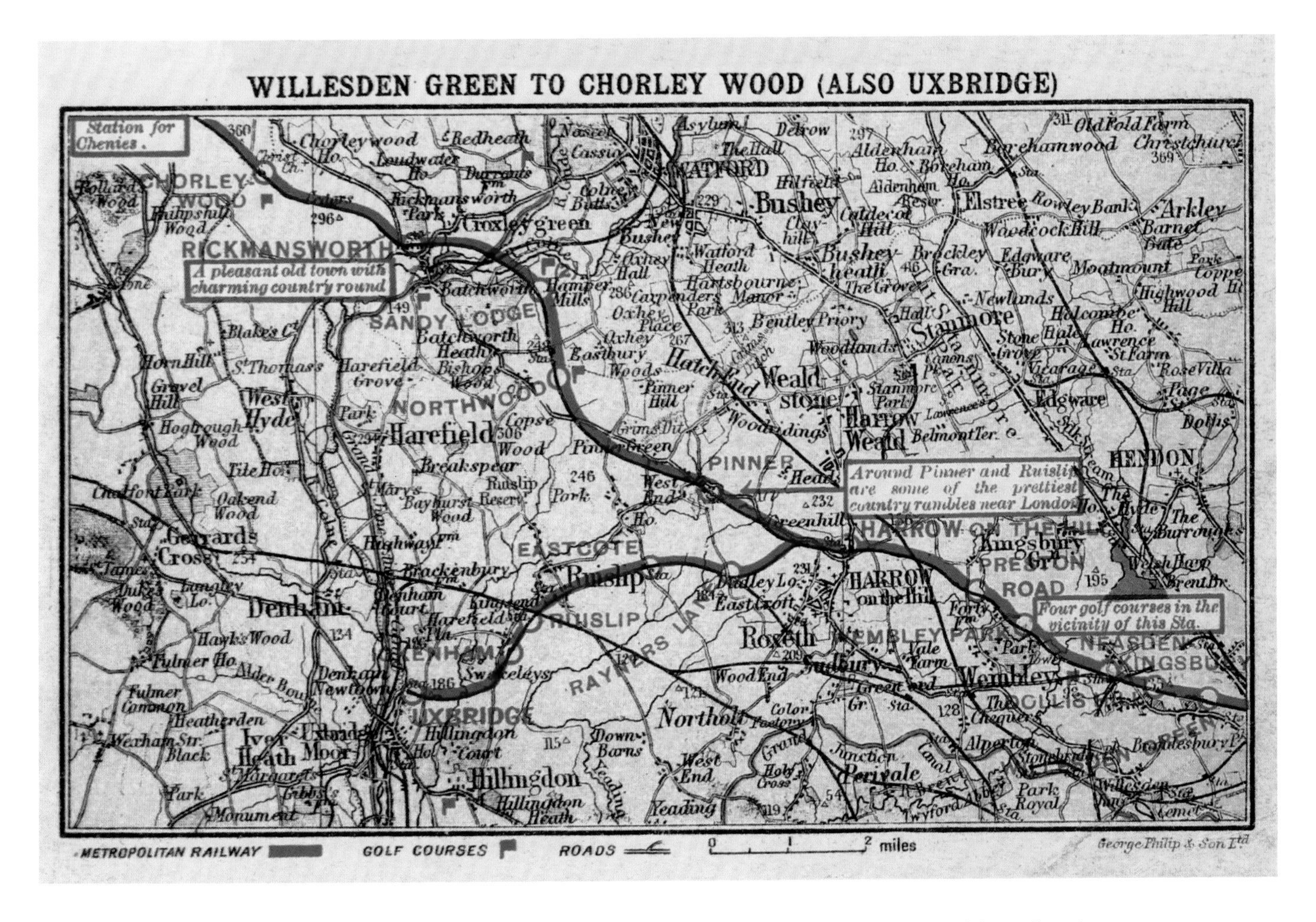

One of the Railway's 1912 map postcards, showing the largely undeveloped sector of the still nameless Metro-land between the outer edge of north west London and south Hertfordshire.

Another type of publicity tool was introduced in October 1909, when the first set of picture postcards of rural scenes served by the railway came on sale. In sepia half tone, they were priced twopence for an envelope of six different views. Four more sets of six were produced in the same year. These were followed in 1912 by a set of six coloured 'Geographical' (map) postcards produced by George Philip & Son, each map depicting a section of the Extension line. Little boxes placed appropriately on the maps carried snippets of information such as 'Around Pinner and Ruislip are some of the prettiest country rambles near London' and at Rickmansworth, 'A pleasant old town with charming country round'. Quainton was shown as 'Noted for its fossils'. Today's postcard collectors pay a minimum of £120 for the whole set of map cards in its original envelope. The year 1909 also saw an extended and updated one penny *Illustrated Guide to the Country Districts*, covering the area served north west of Harrow. Aimed at the rambler and holidaymaker, it contained descriptions of walks and lists of hotels, farmhouses and apartments.

Early in the following year, James Feiron, formerly a timetable clerk, was appointed as the Metropolitan's first Publicity Officer. One of his early steps was to produce a poster advertising five golf courses on the Extension line: Wembley Park, Hillingdon, Northwood, Chorley Wood and Harewood Downs (served by Chalfont Road station). All had 18 holes except the 9-hole Hillingdon.

Feiron's new Publicity Department was soon in fast forward mode. Not only was there the penny Metropolitan & Great Central Joint Railway *Illustrated Guide* with the usual features but a new 96-page booklet called *Near & Far* designed to arouse the interest of home-seekers, a section of society likely to produce a lucrative and steady source of new revenue – potential season ticket holders, especially those investing in First Class season tickets, with wives and children who enjoyed regular visits to the London theatres and the large stores also travelling First Class. Although there were as yet few details and advertisements for new housing, this publication offered information designed to whet the appetite of this select group of the burgeoning Edwardian middle class: a coloured map showing the Underground and another of the whole outer area served by Metropolitan between Baker Street and Uxbridge, Verney Junction and Brill; tables of season ticket rates and ordinary fares; and details of journey distances and times to Baker Street or the City of London. In 1910, a striking poster was widely displayed: *Autumn Foliage in Herts and Bucks* portrayed a double track line in a cutting through chalk. Reproduced from a black and white photograph in a warm sepia tint using an ordinary half tone block measuring 46in by 32½in, it was printed on a heavy cream tone paper within a dark purple border.

In a period when few golfers had access to motor cars, they offered railways a useful addition to revenue which would survive until the 1950s. In 1909 an 18-hole course had been laid out east of the line between Northwood and Rickmansworth and a station was requested. A minimum annual revenue guarantee was sought by the Metropolitan and Great Central Joint Committee and, this given, a cheaply-built halt called Sandy Lodge, with timber side-platforms connected by a footbridge, was then provided at 15½ miles from Baker Street. Opened daily to the public on 9 May 1910, its receipts were very soon well in excess of the guarantee. As we shall see later, from 1923 it also served a new residential development, taking its name, Moor Park.

Sharing publicity costs with the Great Central; the 1910 guide to the territory beyond Harrow.

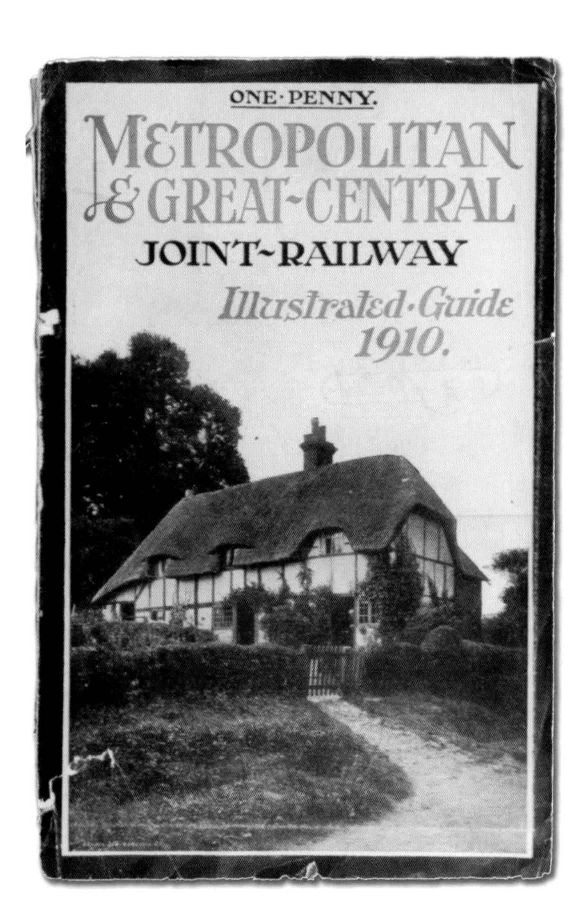

Publicity was sought in a new direction in 1911. On 23 May, Ellis's successor as General Manager, Robert Hope Selbie, who was to do more than anyone else in the next two decades to develop Extension line traffic, gained the Board's approval to order a cinematograph film showing the attractions of the line beyond Harrow. This was to take about a year to complete at a cost of £115 but the picture theatres (then beginning to appear in considerable numbers) would pay a rental for screening it. A copy survived to be used in a 1973 television programme on Metro-land featuring Sir John Betjeman. Two other publicity features appearing in 1911 showed the growing emphasis on residential development along the Extension line. A poster-map *From City to Country Home*, exhibited at every station, depicted the area between Neasden and Verney Junction, showing villages and towns for 6 to 9 miles on the south west side of the line and up to 12 miles on the north east side. Eleven golf courses were indicated on it by red flags. Also appearing from July were the first three issues of *The Homestead*, published quarterly by the Metropolitan and Great Central Railway companies. This contained details of places served by the companies' lines out of London with timetables and much helpful information for the house-seeker. Publication continued in revised versions until the early 1920s.

Guide to the country areas served by the Metropolitan Railway, June 1910, an early attempt to attract the middle class home-seeker. The unsigned artwork suggests an amateur hand.

A 1914 country areas booklet with a cover picture of Latimer. A similar view was used in 1928 as a coloured cover for that year's *Metro-land*, revealing some changes to the cottages in the interim (see page 78).

Walking for pleasure in the fine countryside of the Extension line and its Uxbridge branch had been encouraged since the 1900s, both by convenient cheap ticketing arrangements which allowed outward journeys to one station and return from another, and by a series of pocket-friendly booklets with maps and directions, available for one penny each at all Metropolitan stations. *Country Walks Around London* numbers 18–20 appeared in the autumn of 1912, each booklet containing 26 walks of 6 to 13 miles through Middlesex, Hertfordshire and Buckinghamshire, all planned 'to avoid main roads and their motor traffic as far as possible'. In the new series, Metropolitan walkers were offered the 'picturesque valley of the Misbourn' or the 'far lovelier valley of the Chess', walks into 'a score of romantic villages and half a dozen little country towns'. Readers of *The Railway & Travel Monthly* of August 1912, from which these quotations are taken, were enticed by an offer of a copy of a booklet free of charge.

A note of mild hype was now becoming evident in Metropolitan publicity. An advertisement for Chorley Wood in *The Railway Magazine* for April 1913 spoke of 'fast' trains from Baker Street reaching this station in 45 minutes (an average of 26mph). Here, 'some 400 feet above sea level, consequently in a pure, invigorating atmosphere ... you can readily imagine yourself to be hundreds of miles from London ... The attractions of Chorley Wood are almost inexhaustible and the stranger paying his first visit is astonished at the glorious country provided for him almost on London's doorstep.'

This description daintily treads around the signs of suburban growth the railway had already stimulated. As early as 1903 the Metropolitan had thought it worth while to build for letting a shop (including a sub post office) with living rooms over, on the Down side at the station. The six-inch Ordnance Survey revision of 1913 shows a group of new roads bounded by the railway, Shire Lane and Quickley Lane, containing some 120 new villas. This change was not of course solely attributable to the Metropolitan; here, as at other stations between Harrow and Aylesbury, all traffic was shared with the Great Central Railway after 1899. At Chorley Wood in particular the latter's services will have been equally important in encouraging an increase in residential traffic between 1900 and 1920 (see Appendix 1).

Feiron retired from the Metropolitan Railway in 1914 after 52 years in railway service of which 44 had been with the Metropolitan. He had worked on bank holidays for the previous 51 years and attended every half yearly meeting since 1869. With his departure, Selbie formed a Commercial Department under John Wardle, who had been Goods & Parcels Manager since 1908. Energetic and only 39, Wardle was to include publicity and advertising in his brief and would be assisted in these by another live wire, of whom more in a moment.

Wardle very quickly introduced the abbreviation *The Met* which he also used for the title of a new series of leaflets advertising facilities and services from late 1913. Then, from 1920, he strove hard to have the railway labelled the *Metro*. Neither abbreviation probably appealed very much to his staid and dignified General Manager.

1914 brought three new publications. In the spring *Pastures New* provided guidance for those organising country outings along the Extension line and the Uxbridge branch. *Hedgerow & Hillside* detailed the rural attractions of the same territory, whilst *Country Homes*, published shortly after the outbreak of World War 1, was the first of a free quarterly series (later *Country Homes in Metro-land*), which set out to explain how by use of the Extension line from Baker Street, 'the City man may journey comfortably each day between his place of business and a healthy homestead amid the woods and meadows of the beautiful countryside that lies to the north west of the Metropolis' (*The Railway Magazine*, December 1914). Alas, the rigours and demands of the four years of World War 1 stopped the construction of 'homesteads' in the 'beautiful countryside' and although this booklet continued to appear until at least 1918, it was obliged to concentrate on a limited housing market. Wartime exigencies interrupted its regular quarterly publication at least once.

A quotation from the 8 July 1914 issue of *The Met* entitled 'Unknown Rural Haunts Close to London' perhaps offers a fitting conclusion to this opening survey of our subject, which, until 1915 had no name. In this piece, the reader was invited to:

Below Rayners Lane, as depicted on a carriage interior photograph, pre-1914.

TAKE A TRIP to Eastcote, Ruislip, Ickenham or Uxbridge. In atmosphere, though not in distance, these charming rural hamlets are hundreds of miles away.

GO WHILE NATURE IS FRESH, the birds carolling, the flowers in bloom.

HOW MANY City men know that they can be carried by THE MET straight from their offices into rural solitude where they may wander through fields by lake and thicket in the quiet summer evening, cooled and invigorated by health-giving breezes laden with the fragrance of foliage and flowers?

Step in at Moorgate Street: ask for a return to, say Ruislip (Cost 1/5), and spend a charming time amid trees and fields away from the cares of business and the streets.

FAST – ELECTRIC TRAINS – FREQUENT

An idyllic picture forms in the mind's eye when this is read in the starker environment of the early 21st century; no intrusive noise or exhaust pollution from restless flows of road traffic and aircraft, only the near-silent countryside with its age-old cottages nestling close around Ruislip's ancient parish church, offering summer scents and floral displays in their colourful gardens; no red-roofed 2½-bedroom spec builders' semis to be seen, only a sprinkling of new 'homesteads' (to use a favourite Met term), these discreetly hidden from view. The suburban sprawl is as yet some ten to fifteen years away.

Off then, City man, to Moorgate station, perhaps accompanied by that appealing young Miss Jones from the Office; off by Fast and Frequent electric train to a delightful summer evening in Ruislip …

It seems likely John Betjeman never discovered this invitation, for surely if he had it would have inspired a poem, ending as his work sometimes did on a melancholy note – perhaps reflecting that the 'City man' addressed by the copywriter would all too soon be cheerfully volunteering to fight in the 'Great War to End War', departing for the hell on earth that was the Western Front with a song and a smile, perhaps never to return to ride out to Ruislip again by 'Fast and Frequent Electric Trains'.

3 THE EMERGENCE OF METRO-LAND 1908–1919

Robert Hope Selbie CBE 1868–1930, General Manager Metropolitan Railway 1908–1930; Director Metropolitan Railway 1922–30; Director Metropolitan Railway Country Estates Ltd 1919–1930.

During his period as general manager (1901–08), Abraham Charles Ellis had presided over the important electrification scheme which included the lines from Baker Street to Harrow and those to Uxbridge and South Harrow. He also nurtured the development of an outer suburban traffic, whose significance as an income generator he fully recognised. He was succeeded in 1908 by Robert Hope Selbie, who, building on the sound foundation he had inherited, soon realised that the need to cultivate the Extension line traffic was becoming an even higher priority as motor bus, electric tram and tube railway competition began to eat into the central London and inner suburban zone receipts. Selbie also appreciated the role of publicity and advertising in achieving his objective, setting up, as we have seen, a new Commercial Department under Wardle to include these functions.

By the end of 1912, Selbie had evolved a strategy to maximise outer suburban traffic. His scheme, outlined to the Board, focused on the need to establish a single-minded professional undertaking able to extract the full potential of the railway's territory at and beyond Wembley. He argued that whilst the Surplus Lands Committee certainly had some experience of residential estate development at Willesden Green and Pinner, a new limited liability company should be formed amongst the railway's largest shareholders, this free to concentrate entirely on the creation and successful progress of new housing estates along the Extension line, to be sited both on land already owned and on new purchases. The Board gave approval in principle and steps were then taken towards the purchase of the Chalk Hill Estate at Wembley, of which more later.

Further progress was then interrupted by the outbreak of war in August 1914, but Selbie worked to keep the idea alive, referring to it in an April 1915 Report to the Board. In this, he noted that the important longer distance traffic was 'capable of almost indefinite expansion', pointing to the 'thousands of acres of land ripe for development in building estates immediately adjacent to the line from Neasden northwards and between Harrow and Uxbridge'. The existing statutory powers for dealing with land and the investment of funds were 'somewhat exceptional' but if they were regarded as insufficient to enable the Railway Company to purchase and develop estates adjoining the line 'there is no reason why we should not afford practical help to a subsidiary company to assist in such a business and so add permanently to our own revenue'. As the Railway Company stood to benefit by such development, 'it is in my view essential we should take some practical steps to further this end'.

Part of timetable cover, March 1913, showing a six-car Down electric train approaching Harrow on the Hill station. The old village of Harrow, with its church and famous school, is seen in the background.

As the War continued to drag on, nothing was done but as soon as the Armistice was signed in November 1918, Selbie returned to the subject, suggesting it be 'taken in hand forthwith' to meet the demand for houses after the armed forces had been demobilised. He cited the 'advertisement the districts served have received during the War' a reference to the influx of air raid refugees and the large numbers of service personnel stationed there. Action was duly sanctioned to establish the Metropolitan Railway Country Estates Ltd, in which the Railway Company would take a controlling financial interest; arrangements were made to buy the 123-acre Chalk Hill Estate at Wembley (£22,500) and the 454-acre Cedars Estate at Rickmansworth (£40,000) through a syndicate. Some 40 acres of surplus railway land at Neasden for a third estate and an additional 10.25 acres between Neasden Works and Wembley Park station to enlarge Chalk Hill were also to be sold to the new company for £11,683.

But at the last minute, doubts were raised: Parliament might question a proposal which allowed the railway to buy and develop land for purposes other than railway use without statutory sanction, whatever special provisions had been included in the Metropolitan's existing private Acts. When the opinion of a KC was sought, he advised a court might hold the scheme to be invalid as it was contrary to public policy that a railway company should hold land for other purposes without specific authority. It was therefore thought prudent that the Metropolitan Railway Company as such

H G Gawthorn's attractive cover picture for the first printings of *Metro-land* in 1915–16, artwork which prompted the editor of *The Railway & Travel Monthly* to write of its 'seductive appeal'.

should have no direct interest in the MRCE, but would enter into an agreement with it, allowing use of its name in the new company's title and providing all possible assistance to the MRCE from the railway's organisation towards the development of the new estates. In return, the Metropolitan Railway would have the right to nominate the MRCE chairman and two other directors from its own Board for an initial ten-year period (later extended). It was also agreed that the deposit moneys to be advanced for the initial land purchases should be provided not by the Railway Company but by the underwriting firm Belisha, Shaw & Co, whose Albert I. Belisha was a Metropolitan Railway director. The MRCE came into being on 7 June 1919, with Selbie as a director and all but one of the rest of its Board formed of Metropolitan Railway directors.

The new company was not only given accommodation in the Metropolitan's head offices at Baker Street but the part time services of Henry Gibson, the Surplus Lands Committee's surveyor and valuer and those of other Metropolitan officials, particularly individuals engaged in publicity, advertising and estate duties. Thus from mid-1919, the Metropolitan management was in a unique position among British railway companies in being able to direct a considerable quantity of estate development to sites where it would best serve its interests and also act as magnet to attract independent developers. The MRCE benefited in return from its close association with the railway company's safe and respectable image. 'Railway companies', wrote Selbie smugly in *Modern Transport* (11 June 1921), 'are trusted and not open to the suspicion that often attaches to the speculative builder and estate developer'.

It was in this period that *Metro-land* came into use as a convenient generic term for the exploitable territory served by the Extension line. James Garland, an official and copywriter employed in the Metropolitan Railway's Advertising and Publicity department under Wardle, claimed to be its inventor. He later recalled how, at home early in 1915, fighting influenza, he had leapt out of his sick bed when the word occurred to him. Certainly no use of this term can be found in any Metropolitan Railway publications before 1915. We may assume that Wardle was delighted with it, even if Selbie showed no outward enthusiasm. Its psychological effect should not be underestimated; it was so flexible and convenient to use, not only as a neat label for much of the Railway's linear catchment area but for the ethos of the Railway and its passengers in relation to that area's use, assumed purpose and exploitation.

A new version of the official guide had been under preparation in 1914 but production and printing seem to have been interrupted by wartime priorities. This delay provided opportunity to name it *Metro-land*, perhaps at Wardle's suggestion. As all known copies contain a gummed slip in red print which refers to cancellation of excursion and other cheap tickets '. . . owing to the present war conditions', it would appear that at least some of the type had been set up before the war started on 4 August 1914. And since it was noted as 'a new booklet' in *The Railway Magazine* June 1915, the first copies were probably available in April or May that year. A reprint was required quite quickly; these copies are labelled inside 'Second edition' and bear the printer's mark '30/7/15'. A third printing followed, carrying the printer's inscription '25M–1/5/1916' giving us the issue date and the quantity printed of 25,000. Apart from very minor differences, the contents of the second and third printings appear to be identical and this similarity also probably applies to the first issue, but we cannot be certain as no copy of it has yet been found. The coloured cover used in all three 1915–16 printings shows a young woman picking white flowers in a tree-fringed field.

METRO-LAND
A
PRICE ONE PENNY

The artist was Henry George Gawthorn (1879–1941), who later provided art work for the London & North Eastern and Southern railways. Gawthorn's Miss Metro-land cover, reproduced on a 1915 Metropolitan poster, stirred G. A. Sekon (Nokes), editor of *The Railway & Travel Monthly* to write in his July issue:

> … if some be deaf to the call of nature as depicted by the country, nature in disguise of a charming damsel has powerful attractions for them, so to gather all in the net we have on the green sward of 'Metro-land', a vision fair inviting us to dwell in the district served by the Metropolitan Railway. Which of us will not succumb to one or the other of the two seductive appeals?

At one penny, a third of the cost in 1914 of *The Times* newspaper and twice that of the contemporary *Daily Mirror*, the 80-page *Metro-land*, with its coloured plates, black and white photos and folding double-sided coloured map was something of a bargain. The coloured frontispiece (left) was the 1910 poster mentioned earlier, retitled *The Gateway to the Chilterns*. The tints are appealing but the empty tracks cry out for the addition of a train disappearing on its way deeper into Metro-land.

These early editions of the new annual guide mainly emphasise enjoyment of the countryside, seeking to describe and illustrate the areas at and around the stations from Wembley Park to Aylesbury and along the Uxbridge branch. The outer section,

PULLMAN SERVICE

(WEEK-DAYS)

TO THE CITY.

					SE
	a.m.	a.m.		p.m.	p.m.
Verney Junction …	…	…		…	9 14
Aylesbury ………	8 24	…		4 14	9 46
Stoke Mandeville…	8 30	…		4 20	9 52
Wendover ………	8 37	…		4 27	9 59
Great Missenden …	8 47	9 26		4 36	10 8
Amersham………	8 56	9 35		4 45	10 17
Chesham ………	…	…		…	…
Chalfont & Latimer	9 0	9 39		4 51	10 23
Chorley Wood and Chenies ………	9 4	9 43		4 55	10 27
Rickmansworth ….	9 9	9 48		5 1	10 34
Sandy Lodge ……	…	9 52		5 5	…
Northwood ………	9 16	9 56		5 9	10 41
Pinner ………	9 21	10 1		5 14	10 46
North Harrow……	…	10 3		5 16	10 48
Harrow ………	…	10 10		5 24	10 55
Baker Street ………	9 46	10 27		5 45	11 17
King's Cross ……	9 52	10 32	SE	5 53	…
Moorgate Street….	9 58	10 38	SE	5 59	…
Liverpool Street …	10 0	10 40	SE	6 1	…

FROM THE CITY.

	SE	SO	SO	SE	SE	
	a.m.	a.m.	p.m.	p.m.	p.m.	p.m.
Liverpool Street …	10 11	11 52	1 0	5 25	6 14	…
Moorgate Street….	10 12	11 53	1 1	5 26	6 15	…
King's Cross ……	10 18	11 59	1 7	5 32	6 21	…
Baker Street ………	10 26	12 7	1 15	5 40	6 30	11 35
Harrow ………	10 47	12 25	1 32	5 57	6 47	11 52
North Harrow……	10 53	12 31	1 38	…	6 54	11 59
Pinner ………	10 56	12 34	1 41	6 4	6 57	12 2
Northwood ………	11 2	12 40	1 47	6 10	7 3	12 8
Sandy Lodge ……	11 6	12 43	1 50	…	…	…
Rickmansworth ….	11 9	12 47	1 54	6 17	7 9	12 14
Chorley Wood and Chenies ………	11 17	12 54	2 0	6 23	7 16	12 21
Chalfont & Latimer	11 22	12 59	2 6	6 29	7 21	12 27
Chesham ………	…	…	…	…	…	…
Amersham………	11 30	1 8	2 12	6 35	7 28	12 33
Great Missenden….	11 37	1 17	2 20	6 43	7 35	12 41
Wendover ………	11 46	1 26	2 28	6 51	7 44	12 49
Stoke Mandeville…	11 51	1 31	2 33	6 56	7 49	*
Aylesbury ………	11 56	1 36	2 38	7 1	7 54	12 56
Verney Junction …	…	…	…	…	8 23	…

SE—Saturdays excepted **SO**—Saturdays only.

* Calls if required on Saturdays only to set down passengers, on notice being given to the Guard at the previous Station.

CHARGE FOR ANY DISTANCE . . . . 6D.

POPULAR TARIFF OF REFRESHMENTS.

53

The Pullman service timetable from the April–June 1917 edition of *Country Homes in Metro-land.*

to Brill and Verney Junction, is dismissed in fewer than seven lines. A piece titled 'Pleasure Parties' contains some appealing images. Eastcote, Ruislip and Ickenham are seen as 'nestled for ages amid rural scenery, in summer of almost ravishing beauty' – alas all too soon this was to be destroyed by insensitive speculative development, aided and abetted by the Metropolitan Railway. Pinner is described as '. . . a starting point for pleasure trips through the adjacent beautiful countryside' whilst further out, where the Chiltern district is said to be 'a natural sanatorium', the day tripper in the very early dawn of the great age of motor transport would find Amersham, Great Missenden and Wendover to be 'relics of ancient times undisturbed since the days of our remote forefathers.' Did Garland write this stuff and was it edited by Wardle? We shall probably never know, since the official records are silent on this subject and it seems likely no-one even remotely concerned with the Metropolitan's publications remains alive. At the end of the guide are lists of caterers, of golf courses (reached by the Met's 'rapid, inexpensive, and luxurious' train service) as well as details of country apartments and hotels.

In these early editions of *Metro-land* nothing much is said about the residential attractions of Amersham nor are they advertised. The old town in the Misbourn Valley, whose population had been declining in the period before the opening of the Metropolitan Railway through the area in September 1892, was not directly served by the line, which passed just over half a mile to its north, with a station on the road to Chesham. Hereabouts a whole 'New Town' (later to be known as Amersham on the Hill) appears on the 1923 revision of the six inch Ordnance Survey; given the moratorium on new residential construction arising from World War 1 and its immediate aftermath, this would all have been in place by late 1914. Separate from the old and largely consisting of detached villas, some on plots of one to five acres, along the Chesham Road and new roads east and west, this development was clearly sustained by the railway and apart from some retired and financially-independent residents would have yielded a significant percentage of First Class season and ordinary tickets. Yet in the early *Metro-land* guides it receives scant attention; the 1915–16 scribe briefly and typically goes over the top with 'the brick-red and cream-coloured structures which ornament the grassy hills recall, in their general aspect, the picturesque buildings of the times of Shakespeare and Sir Christopher Wren'. But three years later, Amersham New Town was mentioned in slightly less flowery terms as 'a collection of scattered, cream-walled dwelling houses of picturesque and pleasing design'.

Finally, returning to the earlier edition, we find advertisement pages featuring the delights offered by the Orchard Bungalow and Field at Ruislip, 'An Ideal Resort . . . for School Outings, Bands of Hope and Other Parties' incorporating 'The usual amusements for children' and a 'New Iron Pavilion for Teas, Shelter, &c., seat 500'. Although easier of direct access from London by the District Railway rather than the Metropolitan, The Paddocks at South Harrow offered 30-acre grounds, accommodation for 2,500 at one sitting and 'Very large permanent shelters in case of rain'. Other adverts extolled the delights awaiting parties of children and adults at similar establishments (The Pavilion, Eastcote and The Poplars, Kingsend Farm, Ruislip). All these establishments were doomed to be built over in the ensuing two decades but as yet *Metro-land* contained only two advertisements for housing developments, both within the Metropolitan's control: 'Wembley Park The Ideal Suburb' and the Cecil Park Estate at Pinner. At the latter, no houses were said to be available but applicants would be advised when they were.

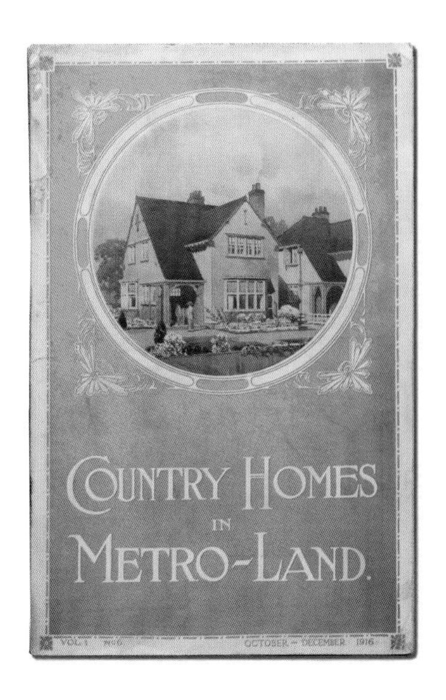

No *Metro-land* annuals appear to have been published in 1917 or 1918 but a number of free booklets with the title *Country Homes in Metro-land* were produced from summer 1915 until 1919, all in a larger format and all with the cover shown above. This one is marked 'Vol.1 No.6 October– November 1916'. Described as 'The Official Residential Guide of The Metropolitan Railway' these booklets contain notes on areas outward from 'Kilburn-Brondesbury', a folding map and a 'Historical Sketch' – all very much on the *Metro-land* pattern. Perhaps the explanation of the change of title had some connection with wartime restrictions but there is no mention of this in surviving official papers.

Although the Great War still raged, morale for those at home or on leave from the Western Front could be temporarily uplifted by a visit to a West End theatre. The Metropolitan Railway was there to help in this. A reproduction from *Country Homes in Metro-Land* Vol. 1 No.8, April–June 1917, which also shows the format of this wartime series (see caption on page 35).

The "Met." Theatre Trains.

HARROW AND BEYOND.

Stations.	Start for Baker Street		
	p.m.	p.m.	p.m.
Aylesbury ..	5.5	—	6.25
Stoke Mandeville	5.11	—	—
Wendover ..	5.17	—	6.35
Gt. Missenden	5.26	—	6.44
Amersham ..	5.35	—	6.53
Chesham ..	—	6.26	—
Chalfont and Latimer ..	5.39	6.35	6.58
Chorley Wood and Chenies	5.43	6.41	7.2
Rickmansworth	5.50	6.46	7.10
Sandy Lodge ..	5.55	—	—
Northwood ..	5.59	6.53	7.17
Pinner	6.3	6.58	—
North Harrow ..	—	7.0	—
Harrow .. arr.	6.7	7.4	7.24
Harrow .. dep.	6.25	7.7	7.37
Baker Street ..	6.52	7.23	8.6

Stations.	Leave Baker St. for Home.	
	p.m.	p.m.
Baker Street ..	11.35	11.45
Harrow .. arr.	11.52	12.12
Harrow .. dep.	11.56	12.15
North Harrow ..	11.59	12.18
Pinner	12.2	12.21
Northwood ..	12.8	12.26
Sandy Lodge ..	—	—
Rickmansworth	12.14	12.32
Chorley Wood and Chenies	12.21	12.39
Chalfont and Latimer ..	12.27	12.44
Chesham ..	—	12C54
Amersham ..	12.33	12.51
Gt. Missenden	12.41	12.59
Wendover ..	12.49	1.7
Stoke Mandeville	A	B
Aylesbury ..	12.56	1.14

A.—Call on Saturdays only providing notice is given to guard at previous station.
B.—Call on Thursdays and Saturdays only.
S.E.—Saturdays excepted.
S.O.—Saturdays only.
C.—Chan e at Chalfont & Latimer.

Take a **THROUGH** Ticket to your Theatre Station when booking.

A MOVING STAIRWAY is provided at Baker Street Station (Metropolitan Railway) connecting with the Bakerloo Tube, enabling passengers to reach Theatres in all parts of the West End with the least possible trouble.

ROUTE **X** Change on to Bakerloo at Baker Street.
Y Change on to Bakerloo at Baker Street and Piccadilly Circus.
Z Change on to Bakerloo at Baker St. & Oxford Circus (Moving Stairway).

April, 1917 COLOUR *Advertisements.* xix

HOUSES IN METRO-LAND

THE above is an illustration of some small

BARN ROOFED HOUSES

now in the course of completion at Wembley Park. They are erected in pairs and have many pleasing features. The snug third sitting room or

GROWLERY

as Dickens would probably have termed it is certainly something novel in homes of this size. The compactness of all the rooms makes the work of the house quite a simple matter, a very important consideration in these times of difficulty in obtaining domestic servants.

The gardens vary in size, some of the plots being as much as 200 feet long, and there is

A CARRIAGE OR MOTOR WAY

running at the back of all the houses so that a car can be kept and heavy goods such as coal, etc., delivered at the rear of the premises.

The houses all contain 3 sitting rooms, combined kitchen and scullery, 4 bedrooms, bathroom, linen closet and excellent sanitary arrangements, and the prices are from £600 Leasehold and £750 Freehold.

No survey charges or legal charges (except out-of-pocket payments) are made.

Immediate possession given on payment of the deposit.

The number of trains daily between Wembley Park and Baker Street and the City is 77 each way. Journey time of fast trains, 12 minutes.

Season Ticket rates, Wembley Park and Baker St., 3 months, 1st class, £2 0s. 6d.; 3 months, 3rd class, £1 7s.

Illustrated booklet will be forwarded to any applicant, and applications for these should be made in the first instance to Commercial Manager, Metropolitan Railway, Baker Street Station, London, N.W. 1. at the same time mentioning this advertisement.

POSSESSION CAN BE OBTAINED ON PAYMENT OF A DEPOSIT AND THE BALANCE EXTENDED OVER A PERIOD OF YEARS AS RENT

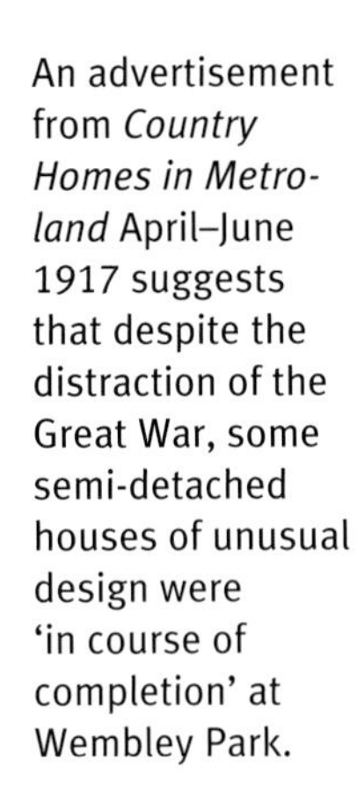

An advertisement from *Country Homes in Metro-land* April–June 1917 suggests that despite the distraction of the Great War, some semi-detached houses of unusual design were ‘in course of completion’ at Wembley Park.

After wartime interruptions, two *Metro-land* publications appeared in 1919, one in midsummer, the second in the autumn. The first, of slightly larger format (8¼ by 5¼ ins), opened with some lines by the veteran journalist George Robert Sims (1847–1922):

I know a land where the wild flowers grow,
Near, near at hand if by train you go,
Metro-land, Metro-land.
Meadows sweet have a golden glow.
Hills are green as the Vales below,
In Metro-land, Metro-land.
Metro-land, Metro-land.

Leafy dell and woodland fair,
Land of love and hope and peace,
Land where all your troubles cease,
Metro-land, Metro-land,
Waft, O waft me there.
Hearts are lighter, eyes are brighter
in Metro-land, Metro-land.

In the Foreword, the reader is informed that the publication has been prepared to 'afford information on what is comparatively a new residential country, and one especially desirable to those who wish to enjoy a rural or semi-rural life amid beautiful natural surroundings, combined with the regular pursuit of their avocations in the City' – yet another 'official' definition of Metro-land, and one which comes close to our own. Seventeen main locations are then paraded in 'Descriptive Notes', illustrated with black and white photographs and some attractive colour plates.

Wembley Park had 'some artistic dwelling-houses, not a great many as yet, but sufficient to show an example for more'; some 20 semi-detached houses were being built for sale at £1,200 each. This estate is given as covering 280 acres, Chalk Hill 123, and both are said to be 'in process of development'.

There was not so much to describe at Preston Road, where prospects 'still remain in the future:- a future composed of residential developments'. This was to prove an accurate prophecy, well on the way to fulfilment when the Metropolitan bowed out in 1933. So for the time being, this was 'pure rural country' [sic] with 'a house or two scattered here and there' enjoying the 'Chiltern breezes which sweep over the hills'.

Eastcote is described as 'a dainty little old hamlet wandering back among the centuries'. Somewhat more alarmingly, the whole district was said to be 'pervaded with a farm-yard atmosphere, which the jaded town-dweller inhales with a sigh of

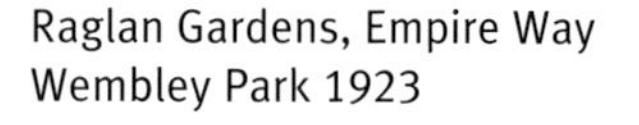

Raglan Gardens, Empire Way
Wembley Park 1923

METRO-LAND
PRICE ONE PENNY

Metro-land reappears in 1919 with a pleasing cover by an anonymous artist and the standard 7ins by 4ins format.

gratitude'. Some readers must have smiled at this strange conception of daintiness, even in 1919. Neighbouring Ruislip had suffered from the events of 1914, when its planned rapid progress as a 'place of residence' with a Garden City and other settlements, was arrested just as they 'were on the point of developing' and 'obliged to remain in a torpid condition ever since'.

Middlesex elms and Edwardian villas on the Ruislip Park House Estate (west of the High Street) c 1910.

Harsh words are then said about the way in which Ickenham, which had 'dozed peacefully through the centuries', surrounded by 'typically English' country of 'great loneliness' had been disturbed by the arrival during World War 1 of an 'enormous aircraft works'. The 'influx of alien influences' was rapidly changing 'the drowsy atmosphere' of the old village.

Pinner was 'now mostly composed of villa residences, with a rural background' but some destruction of its grand elm trees is described as vandalism, which 'it is to be hoped ... will not be repeated'. Alas it was, as we shall see later.

Northwood, completely lacking in 'manufactories', had a 'scattered assemblage of modern residences in their own grounds'.

Passing quickly over Rickmansworth, a town 'rather bare of attractive features', the guide comes to Chorley Wood, where from the station 'one can walk straight into the Fifteenth Century' but had the reader gone the wrong way, he might have encountered a 'group of choice modern residences' attracted by 'Beautiful woods, a glorious open common, and a salubrious atmosphere'.

Not much more was said about new residential opportunities at points beyond Chorley Wood. Beyond Aylesbury the only subject of a 'descriptive note' was Brill, whose 'salubrity ... according to the unanimous opinion of its inhabitants, is phenomenal.'

Edwardian shopping parade in Maxwell Road, close to Northwood station, c 1905.

The section headed *Country Homes in Metro-land* introduces the MRCE, 'whose Board consists of several of the Directors and the General Manager of the Metropolitan Railway Company, with their experts', and adding 'Some of the most beautiful places of residence to be found in England must shortly arise on these Estates'. These developments, the reader was informed with striking honesty:

> ... have been organised, not merely to provide superior houses in rural country near London, but also to create new Passenger Traffic for the Metropolitan Railway. The Metropolitan Railway Country Estates, therefore, are able to *do* more and *give* more than mere ordinary rent-depending properties.'

No doubt seeing this last sentiment in print made the writer feel good, even if it left the reader somewhat bemused. Proposals for the estates were then summarised. At the 40-acre Kingsbury Garden Village (a misnomer, since it was in Neasden and the local authority area was Willesden, but perhaps it was thought to sound better), 40 small houses of different types were in course of erection for sale at £1,200 each. On the Chalk Hill Estate, half and one acre plots had been planned for 'small houses of a country type, with ample grounds for gardens and orchards.' The Cedars Estate at Rickmansworth, covering 450 acres mostly at 360ft above sea level, had some 30 houses 'in course of erection' on plots of half an acre upwards at £2,250 to £7,000 (this last figure is contradicted by a maximum of £3,250 in an advertisement in the same booklet).

Independent building is briefly covered, none of it very significant at this point in time and most of it carried out by local authorities using government subsidies and providing little passenger traffic for the Railway. There were no advertisements for housing developments but features setting out local data, educational facilities, hotels, caterers, country apartments and golf courses were included.

As always, the advertisement pages are of interest. The newly-formed Amersham & District Motor Bus and Haulage Co. advertised circular motor charabanc tours 'throughout the summer months' in the Chiltern Hills, 66 miles in all for 10s 6d from Amersham, as well as their regular bus service from Chesham to High Wycombe. G. Jones & Son of Rickmansworth were less confident of the great Motor Age now emerging, using a photo of their four-in-hand coach and offering 'Brakes, Landaus, Hacks &c., &c ...' as well as motor cars for hire. The guide ended with a folding map of the Extension line showing the Railway Housing Estates and the golf courses and on the reverse, a diagram of lines in and near London, in both cases showing the Metropolitan in red.

Besides the regular features, the 80-page autumn 1919 edition of *Metro-land*, reviewed in *The Railway Magazine* in October that year, reverted to the normal size of 7¼ by 4¾ ins. Its 'Homes in Metro-land' section noted that 'owing to building inactivity during the War and other causes, great difficulty is being experienced in obtaining houses' but the anonymous scribe brightly continues, 'this anomaly, however, will be changed, for through the characteristic enterprise of the Metropolitan Railway, large tracts of land adjoining the Company's system are being vigorously developed as First-class Building Estates.' This was of course a reference to the formation and activities of the MRCE and readers of *Metro-land* were enjoined to 'reap profit by carefully considering the sterling qualities of the estates in question.'

At Neasden, we learn from the guide that 'peace and quiet prevail' (the North Circular Road was still to be built) and 'the stretches of country around afford plenty of opportunity for invigorating exercise'. Here, at 10–12 minutes' journey from Baker Street, the MRCE's 40-acre Kingsbury Garden Village Estate, with its 'rural wayside greens and quaint quadrangles' would contain about 374 small semi-detached houses of 'artistic design' (on another page, the plan is said to be for 'some 384 detached and semi-detached houses'). Using Government subsidies under the Housing (Additional Powers) Act, 1919, construction work eventually began in 1920 after the Board had authorised a temporary siding connecting with the Neasden coal sidings for delivery of building materials. The estate roads (West Way, Village Way, The Rise and Elm Way) were arranged between the new North Circular Road and the Metropolitan Railway staff housing.

Metro-land did not overlook the Railway's Wembley Park Estate, with its adjacent 'finely timbered expanse of some 280 acres' (a section soon to disappear under the stadium and buildings for the British Empire Exhibition). This was being developed 'with the greatest care and its picturesque layout is further advanced by the skilful blending of the varying types of houses'. A colour plate of a small detached villa is included, a doctored version of a black and white photograph of a house in Oakington Avenue first used in the 1917 edition of *Country Homes in Metro-land*.

Also at Wembley, on the MRCE's Chalk Hill Estate, 123 acres of 'charming undulating land' north of the railway, the reader is promised 'small houses, each differing in architectural treatment, are to be erected in plots of an acre upwards.' This estate took the name of a large house on the south side of Forty Lane. Road construction was

Residential Metro-land emerging: Chorleywood West under construction, a 1904 view from Chorleywood Common, looking west.

started in 1920 after the Board had agreed provision of a temporary siding connecting with the existing layout beyond the Neasden Power Station in February that year.

Metro-land then briefly mentioned the Surplus Lands Committee's Cecil Park Estate at Pinner before hurrying on to something more exciting, 'for those who desire pure air, a bracing climate, and rural peace' the MRCE's 454-acre Cedars Estate was 'being developed with the greatest care and there is not even a faint prospect of this charming portion of the countryside emulating the hideous prospects which disfigure so much of Suburban London. Specially-designed residences are to be erected ...' Under the heading 'Chorley Wood', it is stated that the Cedars Estate extended from the eastern side of the Common 'over hill, dale and broad woodlands to Rickmansworth'. Village greens and open spaces were to be provided, with 'unusual stretches of wide and well-made Roads' and also a 'Market Square ... affording facilities for a high-class shopping centre'.

Brief details then followed of independent housing developments already existing in Metro-land but no mention was made of any new construction.

This second 1919 issue of *Metro-land* contained a table of 'Local data of Residential Districts', showing the number of trains each way daily; journey time from Baker Street; local council rates; water charges; range of rents; height above sea level; and type of subsoil. The advertisements section featured no announcements about housing constructed by independent developers, since such activity was virtually non-existent in the immediate post-war years.

4 METRO-LAND ASCENDANT: 1920–30

1920: Metro-land's exploitation launched with a song

The 1920 edition of *Metro-land*, with a new price of twopence, followed much the same pattern as its predecessors. The cover portrayed cottages in Paines Lane, Pinner, a doctored and trimmed version of a colour plate first seen in the midsummer 1919 edition and in uncaptioned black and white photographs in the very first editions. Although this edition noted some minor private building at Harrow and elsewhere (including 34 houses under construction at Eastcote), independent activity was mostly shown as construction or planning of local authority housing schemes, which were assisted by government subsidy.

All the estates directly under Met. control were given due prominence, both in the main text and in advertising panels. Progress had so far been somewhat limited, owing to the many economic and other problems of a nation recovering from a terrible and exhausting war. 'Some twenty semi-detached houses' with three bedrooms and two reception rooms were recorded as being built on plots of varying sizes on the Wembley Park Estate; all were priced at about £1,200 freehold. 'Some 40 small houses of different types' at the same price were said to be in course of erection on the 40-acre Kingsbury Garden Village development at Neasden, whilst the Chalk Hill Estate at Wembley had seen 'a large number of buyers' for house plots of half an acre upwards at £600 an acre.

At the Cedars Estate, Rickmansworth, 30 houses were under construction on plots of half an acre upwards, these priced from £2,250. On the SLC's Grange Estate at Pinner, immediately north of the railway, new roads were under construction and plots from 35ft width upwards were available at £5–6 per foot frontage. It was stipulated that houses should have a minimum value of £1,000, only one to be built on each plot.

Under the heading 'Golf links in Metro-land' no fewer than 15 were now listed. Most had 18 holes, and were situated 'amidst picturesque hills, dales and woods, and possessing every charm that the lover of sport, of clear skies and invigorating air, can possibly desire'. It has to be said that some of these courses were almost two miles from the Met. station mentioned.

This opening year of the new decade also saw the Herman Darewski Music Publishing Company issuing sheet music for a 'Vocal One Step' titled *My Little Metro-land Home*, music by Henry Thraile, words by Boyle Lawrence (see pp 136–142). Someone, perhaps John Wardle, had established contacts in Charing Cross Road – the picture used on the front of the music sheet was a doctored version of the Paines Lane, Pinner picture referred to above.

Live on the Metropolitan

THE range of property included in the area served by the Metropolitan Railway is extensive enough to suit the tastes of the most exacting house-hunter, and the rents and purchase prices likewise vary, so as to appeal to the largest possible public.

Residents in these districts have the added advantage of being able to travel to and from the City without change of carriage, whilst Baker Street is linked up by Escalator with the Underground Electric system, so that there is every facility for expeditiously reaching any part of London.

Foremost among the Building Estates in Metro-land are those owned by the Metropolitan Railway Country Estates, Ltd., and with their vigorous programme of development, house-seeker and investor alike would be well advised to consider the sterling qualities of these unique Estates.

COMMERCIAL MANAGER,
METROPOLITAN RAILWAY,
BAKER ST. STATION, N.W. 1.

Please send fullest information of Houses and Land available in Metro-land.

NAME..

ADDRESS..

....

Opposite The cover of *Metro-land* 1920 presents a prettified view of cottages in Paines Lane, Pinner, doctored further for the sheet music published by Herman Darewski in that year (below).

Left Advertisement in *The Railway Magazine* December 1920.

1921: The railway estates and independent housebuilding make a hesitant start

On 26 July 1921 the Met. entertained a large party of journalists to a conducted tour of Metro-land. Leaving Baker Street at 10.00am in a special train hauled by one of the new 1,200hp electric locos, they visited the Neasden Power Station and Loco & Carriage Works and were given a tour of the adjacent Kingsbury Garden Village, where the recently completed houses were shown. Next came the 120-acre site of the proposed British Empire Exhibition and new Sports Stadium at Wembley Park. On then by train to Rickmansworth, where the party were given a motor coach tour of the Cedars Estate, with two new houses opened for inspection. A lunch was then taken in Rickmansworth, this attended by Selbie and the journalist-versifier Sims, mentioned earlier, who proposed a toast to the success of the Metropolitan, a railway characterised by the three E's – energy, enterprise, and enthusiasm. In reply Selbie made a short speech, in which he expressed the opinion that in developing residential estates, the Company thought they had got hold of a really good thing and were anxious the press should learn about it. He added (no doubt with a smirk) that they also had the capacity to rake in any profits this new enterprise might bring. They had gone beyond any other company in providing houses as well as train services to reach them.

Suitably refreshed, the party then proceeded to Wendover by train, admiring on the way the site of the Cedars Estate either side of the line between Rickmansworth and Chorley Wood. Senses buzzing with the beauty of a still largely unspoiled Metro-land, and filled with admiration for the commercial acuity of the Railway Company, the party was then returned to Baker Street, where their train arrived a little after 4pm, allowing time to file copy for the newspapers' final evening and next day editions. *The Railway Magazine* devoted three pages to the outing, heading its account 'The Metropolitan Railway and The Housing Question'.

Metro-land for 1921 appeared in the spring with a coloured cover picture by C. A. Wilkinson depicting a large gabled and half-timbered house and part of its garden. In addition to the usual features, the 84-page book now included a list of West End theatres. Its 'Country Homes in Metro-land' section surveyed the Railway-controlled estates, where the developers were 'studying to unite to their fullest extent the beautiful in housing architecture to the surrounding beauties of nature' – a noble objective indeed, but alas the 'beauties of nature' would inevitably be damaged and eroded as an ever-increasing number of houses were built in Metro-land. For the time being however, the illusion that these opposing forces could live together in harmony seemed credible, since the colonisation was at first quite gradual.

At the time the guide was prepared, only 30 of the planned 384 houses in Kingsbury Garden Village had been completed and a mere 14 were reported as ready for occupation at Wembley Park. Activity at Wembley's Chalk Hill seems to have been limited to the sale of plots. On the Cedars Estate, 15 houses were 'in the course of erection' with several ready for occupation. The most expensive had six bedrooms and stood in plots of one to one and a half acres. At the Grange Estate, Pinner, plots but no houses were available along the completed roads.

Independent private building enterprise was beginning to make its mark, especially around Harrow, where many plots had been sold before 1915. Albert Cutler, who had started modestly on the Headstone Estate in 1910, was now pushing westward near the railway with his Glebe Estate. This was the precursor of a very large expanse of small and medium-sized semis, all designed for lower middle class Metro-landers anxious to live within a short distance of the two 400ft timber platforms opened as 'North Harrow' on 22 March 1915. Hooking Green, the ancient name for this spot, was swept aside in favour of this obvious topographical misnomer, which was soon applied to the area served as well as the station itself. Cutler's first advertisement in the 1921 *Metro-land* marks a significant milestone, since houses of similar basic plan

C A Wilkinson's impression of a middle class 'homestead' on the cover of the 1921 *Metro-land*.

and size (with limited variations in external appearance) would soon be springing up in significant numbers each side of the Metropolitan between Harrow and Uxbridge. But for the time being, most of the other independent building construction and schemes mentioned in the guide were still government-subsidised local authority dwellings for low income tenants, these not true Metro-landers, since they either did not use the railway at all or paid fares yielding a minimal return to the Company.

1922: Harrow expands both east and west

1922 was the first of the postwar years in which, across Greater London, private enterprise building overtook that for local authorities (who suffered a reduction in government subsidies), this continuing in an unbroken upward trend until interrupted by the economic crisis of 1931. As we shall see, the change was very apparent in the area served by the Metropolitan Railway.

For the cover of the 88-page 1922 *Metro-land*, S. J. Dallaway supplied a coloured picture of another more costly type of 'homestead', in the Company's eyes the ideal architecture for Metro-land, suitable for and affordable only by First Class season ticket holders. In the book's opening pages, there was a further burst of verse from George R. Sims, headed MY METRO-LAND (see opposite).

This edition broke new ground with colour plates to appeal to boys of all ages: one of a 1921–22 electric loco and train; and another of a 1920–21 'H' class 4–4–4T loco. On the railway-controlled estates, there was still not a great deal of activity to report but Cutler again advertised his Glebe Estate at North Harrow, quoting prices from £850 upwards for his boldly bay-windowed semis. There were also two newcomers: Swain & Hunnybun, with their 400-acre Chorley Wood Estate at Loudwater and

Edwardian shopping parade in Station Road Harrow, looking north from a point just by the junction with College Road, c 1923.

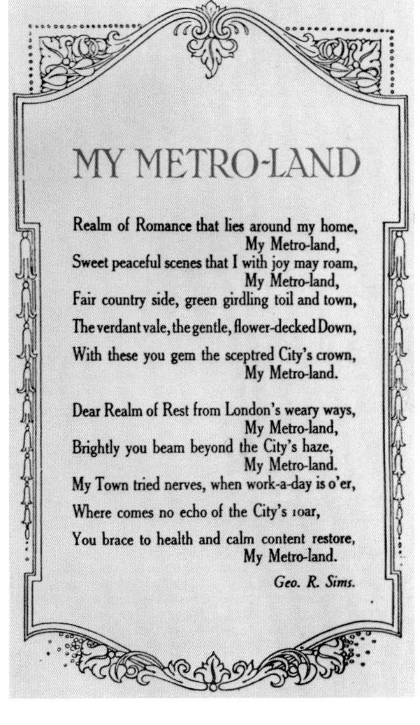

MY METRO-LAND

Realm of Romance that lies around my home,
My Metro-land,
Sweet peaceful scenes that I with joy may roam,
My Metro-land,
Fair country side, green girdling toil and town,
The verdant vale, the gentle, flower-decked Down,
With these you gem the sceptred City's crown,
My Metro-land.

Dear Realm of Rest from London's weary ways,
My Metro-land,
Brightly you beam beyond the City's haze,
My Metro-land.
My Town tried nerves, when work-a-day is o'er,
Where comes no echo of the City's roar,
You brace to health and calm content restore,
My Metro-land.

Geo. R. Sims.

Comben & Wakeling's Manor Estate at Wembley Hill, 'five minutes from Wembley Park station'. On the latter, three-bedroom semis were available at £850–£1,200, four-bedroom types at £1,200–£1,400, and bungalows from £1,000 to £1,250. A table of charges for season ticket rates was now included in the guide to help potential purchasers calculate whether they had enough left for this essential item after paying for the new house and staple items in the family budget.

Northwick Avenue Harrow, looking east, c 1925. The roads here, on the Churchill Estate, were laid out in 1913; the houses, by F&C Costin and others, date from 1920-28. The entrance to the 1923 Metropolitan Northwick Park & Kenton station is seen on the right.

Independent building activity of some significance was also now in evidence alongside and near the line east of Harrow station. Selbie had become aware of preparations for this as early as September 1913, asking for plans to be prepared for a new halt west of the Metropolitan's bridge over the Euston main line. From 1914, south of the railway here, on the 137 acres of Sheepcote Farm, the Hill Golf Club had laid out an 18-hole course together with a nine-hole one for ladies. In 1920, the first houses had appeared in Rushout Avenue on what was known as the Churchill Estate; F. & C. Costin had erected 40 houses here by the end of 1921; all were quickly occupied. Immediately to the north, on the Northwick Park Estate at the beginning of 1922, Walter Jones & Sons had built and sold 20 houses and ten more were under construction. Each of these two estates was planned to accommodate 250 houses. Wardle, investigating the progress of residential building east of Harrow station, told Selbie that residents would prefer to use the Met if a new station were built, since Kenton LNWR station had no direct services to the City. By the end of 1922, he was reporting to his General Manager that 216 houses had been built and occupied in the area; 25 more were in process of erection and 870 more were 'definitely proposed'. This last figure included 500 houses on the Northwick Estate, then in an early stage of development south of Kenton Road and east of the Euston line. Wardle's report ended 'we are losing a lot of traffic', this moving the Board to approve construction of a station on 1 February 1923. No time was lost and Northwick Park & Kenton, with its 420ft long island platform 22ft wide narrowing to 15ft, was opened on the following 28 June, just in time for the Harrow Pageant.

Two new publications appeared in 1922. *Metro-Gram*, a free folded sheet was issued weekly from May; it included details of current and forthcoming events, a theatre guide, a country ramble and 'Two minute Reflections' about railway operation behind the scenes. Within a few weeks it was followed by *Houses in Metro-land*, which had particulars, with plans and drawings, of 'charming residences now available on the Cedars Estate', showing how they might be purchased with a deposit and payments over a period of years. Season ticket rates, train services and local data were also included.

METRO-GRAM

No. 1 Week Ending 20th May, 1922 GRATIS

A WEEKLY BULLETIN OF CURRENT & COMING EVENTS

INTRODUCTION.

THOUGH modest in size, this pamphlet has a big purpose. Each week it will provide the Londoner with particulars of current and coming events, and include, as a regular feature, complete information regarding plays and entertainments. A weekly " country ramble " in the glorious countryside, easily, cheaply and quickly reached by the " Metro," will also add to its usefulness, as will the " Two-Minute Reflections " dealing with divers subjects.

These pamphlets will be published regularly each week throughout the Summer months, and their perusal by the public should prove a useful and entertaining habit.

"WHAT'S ON" GUIDE.

WEEK ENDING 20th MAY, 1922.

Royal Tournament, Olympia, daily.

Cruft's Dog Show, Agricultural Hall, daily.

Travel Exhibition, White City, daily.

Art Exhibition, Whitechapel Art Gallery, daily.

Zoological Gardens, Regent's Park, daily.

Richmond Horse Show, Richmond, May19th.

Opening of Parliament by H.M. The King, May 18th.

Aerial Derby, Hendon, May 20th.

M.C.C. versus Surrey, Lords, May 17th and 18th.

Yorkshire versus Lancashire, Lords, May 19th and 20th.

Meet of Four-in-Hand Club, Hyde Park, May 18th.

Botanic Gardens, Summer Revel, May 20th.

Anglo-American Ball, Albert Hall, May 16th.

Hampstead Hospital Carnival, May 20th.

Royal Tournament, Olympia, daily.

Cruft's Dog Show, Agricultural Hall, daily.

Travel Exhibition, White City, daily.

Art Exhibition, Whitechapel Art Gallery, Daily.

Zoological Gardens, Regent's Park, daily.

Richmond Horse Show, Richmond, May 19th.

TWO-MINUTE REFLECTIONS.

No. 1.—The Romance of a Railway.

Kipling wrote a poem about steamers; another might well be written about trains. We of to-day take our transport facilities as a matter of course, and are resentful if trains, many and swift, are not always ready to convey us whither we would go. Our journey completed, interest ceases, and the wonders of mechanism and organisation that brought that train service into being concern us not. Behind it all, however, there is high romance, and he would be woefully lacking in imagination who, given a peep behind the scenes, failed to thrill to the magic of machinery, to the marvels of electricity in harness, to the ceaseless business of repair, improvement, and acquisition. There is the beauty of perfect efficiency in repair-shop and turbo-room, mystery in the glow of the furnaces, ordered wealth in the store-sheds, and a sense of power over all.

It is proposed in subsequent " reflections " to give the reader this " peep behind the scenes," and show him the " why and wherefore " of railway operation. He will be initiated in non-technical language into the science of power production, be shown how trains are driven, how " rush-hour " traffic is handled, how seconds are saved, how electrically-operated signals work—be shown in fact all that is of interest.

Next Week's Reflection :—
" Through the ' Metro ' Power House."

In May 1922 the Railway began a short-lived weekly leaflet of London events. This is a proof copy of the first edition – inspection of the 'What's On Guide' will reveal some repetition of entries.

The cover of the 1923 edition of Metro-land had the image turned 90° so that one of the new electric locomotives – and the forthcoming electrification to Rickmansworth – could be promoted.

1923: A flood of publicity; and the birth of suburbia along the Uxbridge line

On its cover, the 1923 *Metro-land* featured a photo of electric loco 17 and a train with the caption 'TO METRO-LAND'. The contents were much as usual and Sims' verse *My Metro-land* was printed a second time. The advertising section revealed that Cutler now had houses for sale on the Roxborough and Hooking Green Estates in addition to the Glebe. Other adverts included some newcomers. Halden Estates, developing the surroundings of Hillingdon Court, appear to have had a generous advertising budget, since they took four pages here and had also arranged a full page preliminary announcement in *Homes & Gardens*, September 1922. Halden quickly sought a halt from the Metropolitan to serve Hillingdon Court and its contiguous Hercies Farm estate; this was agreed by the Met subject to a guarantee of net receipts representing a 10 per cent return on the building cost and the additional staff wages bill. A gift of land for a goods yard was a further requirement. Sited on Long Lane, just south of Ickenham village centre, the new station was ready on 10 December 1923. By choosing to call it Hillingdon, the Metropolitan created some controversy since it was well over a mile north of the centre of the old village, but Selbie stood his ground. Gross receipts here in the first year were well over three times the guaranteed sum and by 1930, with around a thousand small houses erected on both sides of the line, they were 20 times higher.

The Halden Estates advertisement referred to on facing page.

Eastcote End Park Estate,

EASTCOTE

THE IDEAL RESIDENTIAL SUBURB.

EMBRACE the opportunity now within your reach of securing your IDEAL HOME amid SURROUNDINGS OF UNSURPASSED NATURAL BEAUTY.

We have here, SITUATION, ARCHITECTURE, WORKMANSHIP, ECONOMY and FINISH to suit every requirement.

This Estate is within 70 yards of Eastcote Station, 12¼ miles from Baker Street on the Uxbridge line.

There is a frequent train service to Baker Street with its connections. You can reach Wembley Park in 13 min., Baker Street 22 min. and Charing X in 36 min.

Harrow with its schools for juveniles is in quite close proximity.

IDEAL fully and semi-detached freehold villas with every convenience, built in spacious grounds are now for sale ready for immediate occupation.

Here you can have your own Tennis Court, Bowling Green and Garage.

Gas, Water and Electricity are at your door. Good metalled roads are already made.

If you desire we can build to your own ideas and design.

Experts are available to advise you on any matter. Mortgages can be arranged.

No would-be owner need fear disappointment.

We have a lifetime's experience in the building trade and are certain we can give you satisfaction.

NO AGENTS. Apply direct to:

TELLING BROS., Ltd.

ESTATE OFFICE, EASTCOTE STATION.

Telephone: PINNER 210. *Now read "Eastcote" Article on page 45.*

SAY YOU SAW IT IN "METRO-LAND."

EASTCOTE END PARK ESTATE

A PAIR OF SEMI-DETACHED HOUSES ON OUR ESTATE.

We have varied types ready for disposal

TELLING BROS., Ltd.

ESTATE OFFICE, EASTCOTE STATION.

Telephone: PINNER 210.

SAY YOU SAW IT IN "METRO-LAND."

Telling Bros. Ltd, the other new advertisers in the 1923 edition of *Metro-land* (above) were developing the Eastcote End Park Estate with houses in Morford Way and Close and some in Hawthorne Avenue, Eastcote, partly on the roads laid out by 1913 mentioned earlier. This was quite reasonably claimed as 'The City Man's Ideal Residential Suburb' since it was within a few minutes' walk of the Metropolitan's Eastcote Halt, although the better-paid City Man might want a more impressive house. As for the 'Surroundings of unsurpassed natural beauty' also mentioned in Tellings' advertisement, these were becoming very vulnerable to further building – Railway Eastcote was under way. In the London *Evening News*, A. V. Lowe was offering three-bedroom semis and four-bedroom detached houses in Lime Grove, Eastcote at £850 and £1,150 respectively. Much more of the same followed.

The *Evening News* also carried advertisements for £100 bungalow plots at Ickenham and, at the other end of the price scale, for the Pinner Hill development by Country Gardens Estates (London) Ltd. Pinner Hill also received publicity and took advertising space in the lavishly-produced monthly *The Ideal Home*. It was a large

Two specially posed photographs show the same train of 'Dreadnought' rolling stock with a Pullman car, headed by a K class steam locomotive of 1925 and electric locomotive No. 10 of 1923. Electrification of the Met reached Rickmansworth in 1925. Steam locos were required beyond until 1962.

gated-estate with plots of half an acre upwards, situated south of Oxhey Woods with views to the south from sites rising to over 400ft. Development proceeded slowly over some ten years from 1923, sales hampered by the 1½-mile distance from Pinner station. This problem was noted in a report to the Metropolitan Railway board in 1929 by Wardle, who was then considering the possibility of the railway running feeder bus services, including one between Harrow, Pinner and Northwood, a proposal not adopted. However, Pinner Hill residents found Northwood Hills station within reasonable walking distance when that was opened towards the end of 1933. From 1928 they also had the solace of an adjacent golf course, planned by Hawtree & Taylor, with its club house in the old Pinner Hill mansion by the ninth green.

C. Hedges used the *Evening News* to announce new detached three-bedroomed houses at £1,275 on the MRCE Chalk Hill Estate at Wembley, where Arthur Marshall & Co. also advertised three-bedroomed semis and detached houses in Forty Lane as 'ready for occupation'. Other adverts revealed that both Telling Brothers and Comben & Wakeling were involved in constructing the Manor Estate at Wembley Park.

Residential Metro-land under way. This c 1930 aerial view of the locality north east of the Metropolitan Railway at Preston Road station was commissioned by F&C Costin as a postcard to advertise their Lyon Farm and Preston Manor Estates, respectively located top right and above Selfridge's Sports Ground. It shows the intermediate stage between open countryside and fully built-up suburbia. Apart from house construction seen in progress in Trevelyan Crescent (right), the other new roads marked in white in the top half of the photo, whilst indicating fairly accurately the final layout, appear to have been added to the original photograph.

The 1923 position on the railway-controlled estates is neatly summarised in a four-page leaflet *Country Homes in Metro-land*, issued during that year. At Kingsbury Garden Village, all 40 houses built had been sold but plots were still available. At the Rickmansworth Cedars Estate, only two of the completed houses remained unsold; on plots of one and one and a half acres these were priced from £3,000 freehold. At the Grange Estate, Pinner, the leaflet informs 'a scheme of development is progressing' but nothing is said about any new house building at Wembley Park or Chalk Hill, despite the newspaper advertising just mentioned.

Through most of the 1920s Preston Road was busiest in the summer months, with golfers and the staff of London business houses travelling to and from the several large sports grounds in this district. Selfridges had purchased 15½ acres between the railway and Woodcock Hill Lane in 1922 for use by its staff and apart from wartime requisition this facility was a social centre for the store's employees until sold in 1958. Tea rooms were built in 1923 and a very impressive new pavilion in 1924. Previously this site had been used for the same purpose since 1912 by Marshall & Snelgrove, the Oxford Street store, then briefly by Lloyds Bank and Debenhams. There were other similar grounds, including those of W. H. Smith & Sons (located east of Selfridges) and the United Dairies and Associated Newspapers, these last two south of the railway. From 1922, Metropolitan Railway employees had sports and recreational facilities north of the line between Wembley Park station and Forty Lane.

A hang-up calendar for 1923, believed to be the first of a series, bore a reproduc-

A constant reminder to all passengers: the *Metro-land* slogan engraved below the inside door handles of the Railway's T stock compartment coaches.

tion of the 1922 *Metro-land* cover and below it, a monthly tear-off pad with a 'Metro Message' underneath. A map of London was printed on the reverse side. Another publication, mentioned in advertisements in *The Railway Magazine* for June and August 1923, was *Homes in Metro-land*, obtainable from the Commercial Manager for 2s 6d post free. At this relatively high price, the handbook offered 'exclusive' designs and plans for 42 houses and bungalows, with many illustrations in colour, tone and line. These could be erected on plots at the Cedars and other estates. Just to confuse, the same title was used for a contemporary 16in by 21in white paper 'broadsheet' advertising a variety of Metro-land properties priced between £750 and £2,500.

A new copywriter, signing simply as 'F.' was engaged in 1923 to wax eloquent on the subject of Metro-land. An early, perhaps the first, specimen of his highly-charged eulogistic prose appeared in an eight-page free booklet printed in that year (see pages 58 and 59).

In producing this flood of publicity, some of which may have been prepared ready for distribution or sale at the 1924 British Empire Exhibition at Wembley, Wardle and his staff did not overlook the rambling fraternity. In the summer of 1923, numbers 51–54 of *Country Walks in Middlesex, Hertfordshire and Buckinghamshire, Metropolitan & Great Central Railways* appeared in brightly-coloured wrappers. Measuring 9¾in by 4in, they were a convenient size for the 1923 male leisure jacket pocket. Each contained 22 pages of print, an index and space for notes. These twopenny booklets, sold at all stations, were advertised by a 40in by 23in poster.

Two pages from an eight-page free booklet issued by the Met in 1923.

METRO-LAND

FEW years ago Londoners were offered a new word—Metro-land. They adopted it at once, and though the gazetteers may not recognise it, it is now part of the living speech of men. Metro-land is Middlesex in one part, Herts in another, and Bucks in a third. Those who dwell within its borders pay their rates and taxes in those particular counties, but their homes are in Metro-land.

The precise boundaries of Metro-land are a little elusive. No one quite knows where Metro-land really begins—how far exactly beyond the long tunnel which forms the dark avenue of its approach from Baker Street. Does Metro-land begin at Willesden Green ? I should rather guess Neasden or the pleasant slopes of Dollis Hill. But the cross roads by Blackbird Farm, and the old church at Kingsbury above the lake-like reservoir, standing in the square camp which the Romans made, before London was, these certainly belong to Metro-land.

Then take a stretch of country five or six miles wide on either side of the shining rails and follow on past Harrow and Rickmansworth, and through the Chilterns, and out into the vale beyond, and all that lies to right and left beyond Aylesbury to Quainton and the Claydons and Verney Junction, where London is far out of sight and mind, all this is Metro-land. It is a strip of the Home Counties and for charm and beauty, its like is hard, its superior harder still, to find.

What is the particular charm of Metro-land ? It is not "violently lovely," as Byron said of one of his early loves, but, like her, it "steals upon the spirit like a May-day breaking." Its charms are many and varied. Middlesex, where it still contrives to escape the fast-spreading tide of London, wears a pleasant homely face. The elms grow tall in its fields and pastures and in the broad plain that stretches below Harrow's airy ridge towards Uxbridge.

Harrow-on-the-Hill, crowned by church and school, is the capital of this Riding of Metro-land ; Ruislip and Northwood are its lake district ; Eastcote and Ickenham, Harefield and Pinner are its rustic townships. London is at your very door, if you needs must keep in touch with London, but it is always pure country at the corner of the lane beyond your garden fence. The town has stained the country less here than in Essex, Kent or Surrey, at the same radius of ten or twenty miles from Charing Cross.

But for many the best of Metro-land begins where the iron road starts to climb in among the Chilterns, which are the very heart of Metro-land—the flinty Chilterns with their tangled ridges, their stony yet fruitful fields, their noble beech woods and shy coppices, their alluring footpaths, their timbered cottages, scattered hamlets and pretty Georgian townships strung out along the high roads.

I know no more dainty group of little country towns than Rickmansworth, Amersham, Chesham, Missenden, and Wendover, leading on to the fine old market town of Aylesbury—English to the core—each with its ancient church, its old manor-house, its picturesque inns, and its exquisite setting of hill and wood. I know few more charming villages than the twin Chalfonts, Latimer and Chenies, Little Missenden, Penn, windy Cholesbury, the Hampdens, Great and Little, the Kimbles, and a score of others that might be named. Few streams run a brighter course than the Chess, and where will you find woods more delightful than those of Shardeloes and Penn, Hampden, Chequers and Halton ?

Only a narrow tongue of "homely, hearty, loving Hertfordshire" lies in Metro-land, but within its pale are Rickmansworth and its lovely parks, and here is the waters-meet of Chess, Gade and Colne. Rickmansworth is a delightful old-world town, and Chorley Wood Common flames into yellow gold when the gorse is in flower.

Historical associations from the earliest times, camps and earthworks, old churches, old cottages, old inns, and a pleasant, simple country-folk to talk to, good roads, good paths and quick change of scene and view—Metro-land falls short in nothing which the heart of man can desire.

Are you in search of views ? Then follow the line of the Chilterns where they rise steeply above the vale of Aylesbury on either side of Wendover from Tring to Risborough, and you shall have views that will linger sweet in the memory. Or try the views from Oving and Pitchcott, beyond Aylesbury, or climb to the little town of Brill, which is another Shaftesbury, so cunningly is it set towards all points of the compass. And if there are meadows where the grasses grow richer, and the may-trees throw a sweeter perfume on the air, than those of Aylesbury towards Hartwell and towards Eythrop, I know them not.

Metro-land—the land which the Metropolitan Railway is proud to serve—is a strip of England at its fairest, a gracious district formed by nature for the homes of a healthy, happy race,

F.

THE NORTHWICK ESTATE

NORTHWICK PARK & KENTON

LONDON'S NEW SUBURB

9 miles from the Marble Arch.
14 minutes from Baker Street.
Served by three Electric Railways.
Over 100 Trains each way every day.

A UNIQUE SPECIMEN OF TOWN PLANNING

The Largest and best laid out Estate near London.

Delightful & Artistic Freehold Houses for Sale

Each a distinctive Ideal Home in every sense of the word.
Splendidly built, only the best material being used.
Perfect rural surroundings, Lovely views, Extraordinarily healthy.
Well constructed Roads. Main Drainage. Electric Light and Gas, and Colne Valley Water.

WOODCOCK HILL LANE.

SAY YOU SAW IT IN "METRO-LAND."

106

THE NORTHWICK ESTATE

NORTHWICK PARK & KENTON

A New and Exclusive Residential District

A PROSPECT TOWARDS STANMORE.

A FEATURE OF THE ESTATE is the fact that **Unusually large Gardens** are provided, the average depth allowed elsewhere for the modern house and garden is 115 to 120 feet, whereas here the minimum depth is 170 feet; the density of houses per acre including roads and open spaces being about 4·5, whereas on most estates developed by modern builders the density averages from 12 to 15.

Property on this Estate cannot depreciate in value.

"THE PALAESTRA"

The Estate Recreation Ground of 5 acres in extent, laid out by the Permanent Hard Tennis Court Co., provides both Hard and Grass Courts, Bowling Green and Children's Playground. The picturesque Club House provides first-class dressing accommodation, Tea Lounge, Concert and Dance Room.

Illustrated brochure and plans and specifications of houses may be had from the Surveyors to Lord Northwick's Trust Estates:

MESSRS. NICHOLAS,
4 ALBANY COURT YARD, PICCADILLY, W.1.
Telephone - - REGENT 293 & 3377

. . . *and* . . .

THE NORTHWICK ESTATE OFFICE,
KENTON RD., NORTHWICK PARK, Nr. HARROW
Telephone - - HARROW 1031

SAY YOU SAW IT IN "METRO-LAND."

107

1924: Suburban Metro-land's expansion starts in earnest

The calendar for 1924 featured a colour picture, *Autumn in Metro-land*. Even here, a reference to a willingness to supply information on residential development and related data was not overlooked.

Expanded to 118 pages to accommodate information on the delights of the British Empire Exhibition at Wembley, the 1924 *Metro-land* cost threepence. Its cover (page 62) by C. A. Wilkinson portrayed the new Stadium and the Exhibition section occupied pages 11–24. This was followed by a new ten-page feature, 'How to get About London' which included information and maps showing the location of the main railway termini, theatres and music halls, buildings of historical interest and museums. This section was to be continued and expanded in later editions. Ever optimistic, the Publicity Office over-estimated demand, leaving some 15,000 surplus copies of the 1924 *Metro-land* in the stockrooms by October. Selbie agreed to a suggestion from Wardle that this overflow be distributed to London County Council Schools.

A major event of 1923–24 relevant to Metro-land was the start made on transforming the Moor Park estate on the Metropolitan & Great Central Joint Line between Northwood and Rickmansworth into a new residential area with extensive sports facilities. We have already noted the opening in 1910 of a golf halt here. In 1919, Lord Ebury's 2,935-acre estate each side of the line was purchased by Viscount Leverhulme, soapmaker and philanthropist, who then sold much of it on to Moor Park Ltd, a new company formed primarily to develop two more golf courses and an up-market residential estate west of the railway, a development which bid fair to generate a modest but highly lucrative traffic.

From 18 October 1923, the name of the station was changed to Moor Park & Sandy Lodge. Two freight sidings were laid on the west side, south of the platforms, in September 1923 but were not available for full public use until June 1925. Construction of new roads was followed in autumn 1923 by a start on building substantial detached houses designed by George E. Clare. These had four to five bedrooms with up to three reception rooms and were priced between £2,500 and £3,000. A contemporary brochure claimed they were 'constructed to last a century without the need for anything more than minor repairs'. At the station, a new approach road on the west side of the line was completed in 1924 and *Metro-land* that year carried the first advertisement for the residential area. Assisted initially by temporary 60cm gauge railways and the new sidings, road and house construction then continued through the 1920s and beyond, gradually filling up the old private estate west of the railway apart from the new golf courses.

Other new building developments advertised in the 1924 *Metro-land* included: Messrs. Nicholas at Woodcock Hill Lane, Northwick Park Estate (illustrated left); C. W. Simmonds and Horace J. Hewlitt, Kingsbury Hill, Blackbird Farm Estate; and Economic Estates Ltd, Chorley Wood Common Estate.

A booklet issued free in 1922-23 to promote 'pleasure traffic' in *Metro-land*. Note the use of Wardle's 'Metro', reluctantly tolerated by Selbie in publicity but he would not allow it to be added to station name signs at street entrances.

AT CHORLEY WOOD.

AT PINNER

AT CHENIES

AT RICKMANSWORTH.

A much wider choice was now becoming available to intending purchasers of a Metro-land home. *Evening News* advertisements during 1924 show new developments at Pinner Road, North Harrow (A. Cutler, with three bedroom semis at £750, four bedrooms £950); at Woodside Avenue, Chesham Bois, £675; at Swakeleys Deer Park, Ickenham (£750–£950); at Harlington Road, Hillingdon Village (three-bedroom bungalows (£450–£525) and also at Hillingdon, the Parkwood Estate, with semis at

£900 and plots from £90. At Ickenham village, Drummonds were building semi-detached bungalows to be sold at £670, whilst plots here were to be had for £75. Adjoining Wembley Park station, Claude Bastable was offering semis at £1,000; and just south of Preston Road station, facing the golf course, C. Burrage had built large semis at £1,400. These had views over the golf course, soon enough to to be exchanged for another vista – of new houses.

KINGSBURY HILL ESTATE

(BLACKBIRD FARM)

Few minutes from Wembley Park Station, whence 10 minutes to Baker Street
General Bus Service No. 8B passes Estate.

A beautiful residential estate of over 100 acres, situated amidst charming rural scenery yet less than 6 miles from Marble Arch.

FREEHOLD BUILDING SITES available at £4 10s. per ft. frontage.

ABSOLUTE TITLE. FREE CONVEYANCE.

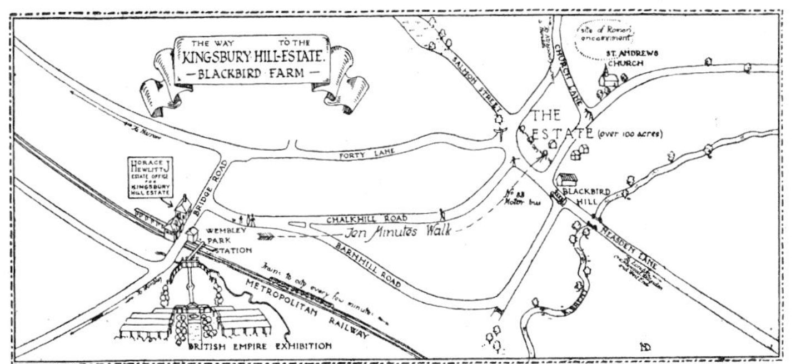

BUNGALOW & VILLA RESIDENCES from £750 to £3,000

Designed and erected to purchasers' requirements on easy terms of payment.
Sewer, Water, Gas and Electric Light.

Apply to Freeholder & Builder—

C. W. B. SIMMONDS

69 EXETER ROAD
CRICKLEWOOD, N.W.2.
Phone - - - Willesden ONE.

Sole Agent & Surveyor—

HORACE J HEWLITT

Queen's Park Stn. Phone Maida Vale 1010.
Wealdstone Station - Phone Harrow 773.
Kenton Station - Phone Harrow 994.
Hatch End Station - Phone Hatch End 149.
Wembley Park Stn. Phone Wembley 1707.

SAY YOU SAW IT IN "METRO-LAND."

111

Simmonds' advert in the 1924 edition of *Metro-land* for the Kingsbury Hill Estate, quoted on the map as ten minutes walk from Wembley Park station. The map also shows the temporary exhibition station at Wembley Park on the east side of Bridge Road.

This 1925 poster, with its picture of Watford Market Place, deceitfully suggested the new railway terminated in the town centre. (No effective complaint could be made since the Advertising Standards Authority did not exist until 1962). At least one of these posters survived World War 2 salvage and subsequent pulping to be sold at Christie's in 2004 for £1,792.

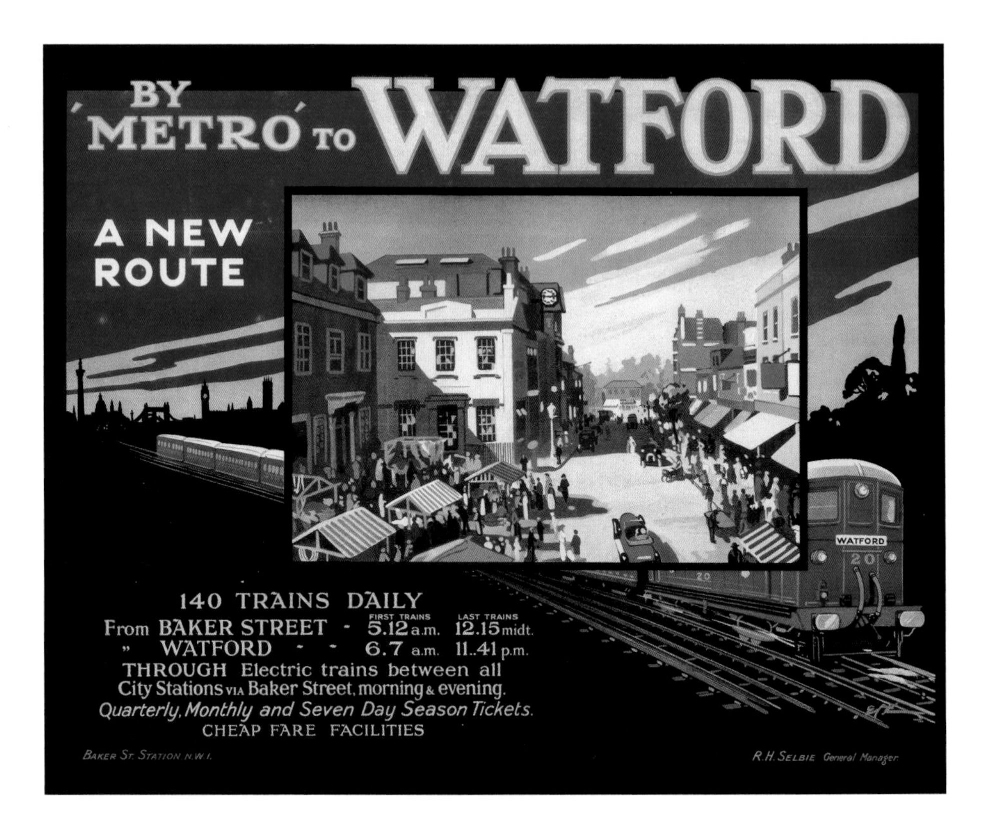

1925: Electrification opens up central Metro-land

From 5 January 1925, electric trains ran between Harrow and Rickmansworth and from 2 November over a new branch through Croxley Green to Watford, this shared with steam trains of a none too enthusiastic London & North Eastern Railway. In 1912, Watford Council had neatly nipped this project's prospects in the bud by securing abandonment of its final section into the town along the southern edge of Cassiobury Park, a move which left the Metropolitan and its partner with a remote terminus on the western edge of the built up area. The LNER trains to and from Marylebone were not well patronised, ceasing with the outbreak of the 1926 General Strike, never to return.

Crippled as it was by a poorly-sited, if handsome, Watford terminus (designed by Charles W. Clark, the Metropolitan's in-house architect), the arrival of the new line was marked by a burst of publicity. A souvenir booklet in a blue cover, *Watford's New Railway*, was issued to the guests at the opening ceremony on the Saturday before public service began. A convenient card folder, *Metro and LNER*, *Watford's New Railway*, dated 2 November 1925, listed every train operated over the line by each company and gave details of season ticket rates. Wardle also arranged a full page advert in *The Watford Observer*, headed *Watford's New Railway, Metropolitan and LNER Joint Effort*. Above this was a drawing of a Met electric train and an LNER steam service running alongside. A folded broadsheet *Watford Homesteads Served by Metro*, giving residential details, appeared in March 1926.

The calendar for 1925, which continued in the same format, used the cover picture of the 1924 *Metro-land*. This item was available from Wardle's office on receipt of a threepenny stamp.

A 118-page *Metro-land* appeared in midsummer 1925. Although still giving information on the Wembley Exhibition held again that year, the price went back to twopence, remaining unchanged until the last edition in 1932. Once again the cover, by C. A. Wilkinson, depicted a 'homestead' of some size and substance, likely to be accessible only to the moderately wealthy First Class season ticket holder. The feature 'Country Homes in Metro-land' noted that the Railway's residential estates now covered 630 acres. 'Well-known firms of builders' were continuing operations at Kingsbury Garden Village and three-bedroom, two-reception room houses could be secured for £950 upwards. The MRCE had built shops at Wembley Park, each with a self-contained flat above, a combination priced at £2,500. On the 120-acre Chalk Hill Estate at Wembley Park, plots were available at a minimum quarter acre for £75. A few plots remained at Cecil Park, Pinner and on the adjacent Grange Estate, many more were available. On the Cedars Estate, 'detached residences of the country house type and bungalows of artistic design', were arranged along 'wide and well-made roads'. Plots were still available here at £650–£800 an acre. Cheaper sites were also for sale south of the railway and adjoining Chorley Wood Common.

The residential attractions of Wembley, particularly the area around Wembley Park station, certainly received a significant boost from the British Empire Exhibitions held in the old Tower Park in 1924 and 1925. Study of contemporary photographs suggests a high proportion of exhibition visitors were in the social and age groups likely to include househunters. They would have rightly been impressed by the public transport accessibility of the area, with its sixteen railway stations, many with electric trains, offering travel times to and from central London in around a quarter of an hour, these supplemented by excellent electric tramway and motor bus services enabling new home owners to keep in close touch with relatives and friends in the older inner suburbs.

Widenings and other improvements had been made in the rural road system to facilitate bus and car access to the Exhibition, these works funded by the Ministry of Transport, the county and district councils and the Exhibition promoters. As the visitors arrived at Wembley Park station or approached the Exhibition along the newly-widened Forty Lane and the two-year old North Circular Road, building activity on the new Haymills Barn Hill and other estates would be in clear view, as would the still apparently rural nature of much of this sector of Metro-land. Having purchased the Barn Hill estate in 1923, Haymills (active in Hendon since 1905) had made a start on an ambitious scheme to build over the south and south western slopes of this 281ft gravel-topped clay hill. The first houses, detached with three to five bedrooms, in Corringham Road and the lower parts of Barn Rise and Barn Hill, also in Grendon Gardens and Eversley Avenue were to be had for £1,275–£2,000 from 1925. Haymills also built the Grand Parade shops in Forty Avenue in 1928–29.

Nearby, Comben & Wakeling were offering three-bedroom semis at £750–£1,000 and four-bedroom types at £1,100 to £1,250 'in the bracing air and rural delights' of the Park Lane Estate, 'nearly 200 feet above sea level'.

Somewhat less appealing was an advertisement by the Woodside Estate Co. Ltd, with two photos of closely-spaced bungalows and semis along unmade roads at Chesham Bois, priced at £735 upwards.

Advertisements in the *Evening News* reveal other active sites at this time: Cramb Bros. at Wellacre Road, Northwick Estate (four bedrooms £1,550); Horace J. Hewlitt at Byron Road, Harrow (£630–£975) and also at Harrow, the Chandos Estate at Buckingham Road (semis at £899 from Granville Howard & Co.) and Woodlands, Pinner Road (Sharp's semis at £815–£895). At Ruislip Manor, Kingsend, Pinn View, four-bedroom houses were available at £1,085 freehold. Those buying houses on the Cassiobury Park Extension Estate at Watford from Charles Brightman & Sons Ltd needed to consider a minimum of £995 but enjoyed the advantage of living only a few minutes' walk from the new Watford station.

BARN HILL ESTATE WEMBLEY PARK

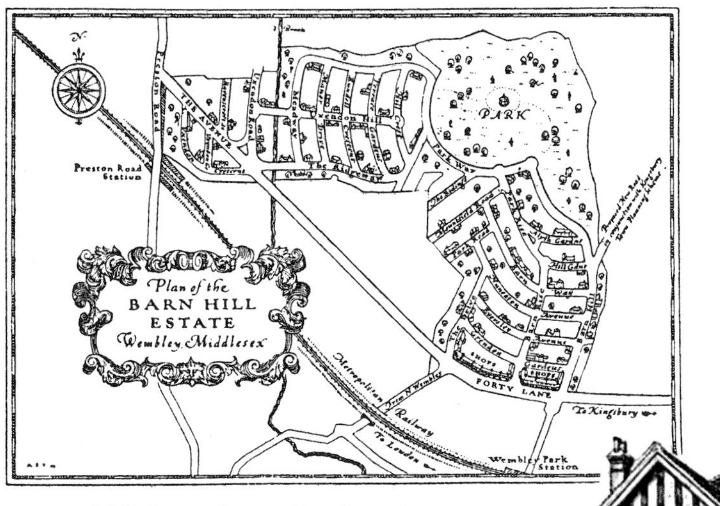

280 feet above Sea-Level

Situated on the Southern and Western slopes of Barn Hill in the health-giving air of the open country, Barn Hill Estate promises to be one of the most attractive and convenient residential estates in N.W. London. More than 1000 detached houses containing 3, 4 or 5 bedrooms are being built.

44 acres are reserved for a Public Park. Every house will have a good garden back and front and space for a garage. Shops are being erected on the borders of the estate. Golf and Tennis Clubs are within easy reach.

10 Minutes from Baker Street

Preston Road and Wembley Park Stations adjoin the Estate. The new arterial road affords motorists direct communication with London and all parts of the country.

Rates 5/2d. in the £ for half year. Main drainage. Colne Valley Company's water.

Visit Barn Hill Estate

and inspect the houses in course of construction. The Estate Office is within sight of Wembley Park Station, and representatives are in attendance daily, including Saturdays and Sundays.

Gas and Electric light to all Rooms. Space for Garage included in purchase price. Interior decorations finished to purchaser's choice.

Prices from £1275 to £2000

(Leasehold and Freehold).

Easy terms of purchase can be arranged.

Write for Booklet

giving particulars, plans and prices of the various types of Houses being erected, and other most useful information. Free on request.

HAYMILLS, LTD
BARN HILL ESTATE
Wembley Park, Middlesex

HAYMILLS HOUSES

SAY YOU SAW IT IN "METRO-LAND."

117

An early announcement of Haymills' Estate on the southern slopes of Barn Hill, above Wembley Park station (from *Metro-land* 1925).

At Moor Park, 'Perfect modern homes in a fine old timbered park' were advertised in the 1925 *Metro-land* under an eye-catching black and white drawing by Fred Taylor RI (1875–1963), who produced art work for the Underground and the Metropolitan Railway as well as all four main railway companies.

Perfect modern homes in a fine old timbered park

In the pure upland air of Moor Park you may choose your perfect home and pay for it upon convenient terms . . . . A home equipped with every known device for your comfort and convenience. You may see such houses any day for yourself . . . . . They are here awaiting your occupation.

Great expanses of greensward and woodland are yours to roam at will. Tennis courts, croquet lawns and three 18-hole golf courses call you to stretch your limbs . . . . Or, if you would laze, there is a stately eighteenth century mansion for your country club.

Come . . . . . Moor Park Station on the Estate is but 26 minutes from Baker Street or Marylebone, and if you first ring up Rickmansworth 217, we shall be glad to meet you and take you round. Failing this, write for an illustrated booklet to

Estate Manager *MOORPARK* *Hertfordshire*

SAY YOU SAW IT IN "METRO-LAND." 112

SAY YOU SAW IT IN "METRO-LAND." 113

Two other adverts from *Metro-land* 1925.

HARROW and KENTON.

The House "De Luxe."

IT ONLY NEEDS INSPECTION TO APPRECIATE ITS SUPERIORITY.

£1,200 Freehold to £2,500 Freehold
£1,025 Leasehold to £2,250 Leasehold

SPECIAL FACILITIES FOR EASY PAYMENTS

DESIGNED for Comfort, Convenience and Economical upkeep. Hall, 2 Reception Rooms, 3, 4 and 5 Bedrooms, combined and separate Kitchens. Bathroom and Scullery Walls Tiled, and all modern improvements. Good Cupboard accommodation. Large Gardens. Room for Garage with every house.

Reinforced Foundations.
Solid walls throughout, no Lath and Plaster.
Two New Stations on the Estate.
Expresses, City (25 mins.) & West End (15 mins.).
Few minutes best Shopping Centre.
Rates 5/1 half-year.
Water, Gas and Electric Light laid on.

CAN BE VIEWED AT ANY TIME.

Golf Links and Sports Grounds adjoin Estate.

Offices:

F. & C. COSTIN, Dept. "G," Builders & Owners, Station Rd., Harrow.
PHONE: HARROW 1100 & 1101.

SAY YOU SAW IT IN "METRO-LAND." 108

PINNER & HARROW

A Superior House for the man with a moderate Income

£900 and upwards Freehold.
£750 and upwards Leasehold.

SPECIAL FACILITIES FOR EASY PAYMENTS.

SEMI-DETACHED designed for comfort, convenience and economical upkeep, comprising Hall, Living Room, Drawing Room, combined Kitchen and Scullery, three Bedrooms, Bathroom and separate W.C. Good cupboard accommodation and all modern improvements. Large garden.

Low Rates. *Fast Train Services.*
Near Metro., Bakerloo, and L.M. & S. Rly. Stns.
Water, Gas, and Electric Light laid on.

OFFICES:

F. & C. COSTIN, Builders & Owners
(Dept. "T")
STATION ROAD, HARROW.
Phone: HARROW 1100 and 1101

SAY YOU SAW IT IN "METRO-LAND." 109

A page from the 1925 commemorative booklet produced by the Metropolitan for the opening of its extension to Watford. This house on the Cedars Estate, Rickmansworth, was designed by the Met's own architect, C.W. Clark.

Architect, C. W. Clark.

RESIDENCE ON CEDAR'S ESTATE, RICKMANSWORTH.

HOUSING DEVELOPMENT IN METRO-LAND.

IN view of the Estate developments which have taken place in Metro-land and the additional facilities which are now being provided by the extension of the electrified line from Harrow to Rickmansworth, it will not be out of place to give some indication of the active housing development that is taking place in Metro-land.

The Metropolitan Railway Company has, principally by the excellent train service between Metro-land and Baker Street, and the City, and through its affiliated Land Companies been able to develop several large Estates on those portions of the land nearest to town, and on these have been built, amid charming surroundings, a large number of houses which combine beauty with utility.

The principal Estate now being developed is the Cedars Estate, 500 acres in extent, which is notable for its delightful situation and for its abundance of charming features, and no more delectable spot could be desired as a place of residence. It is undulating in character; possesses a subsoil of gravel, sand and chalk; is conveniently situated near Rickmansworth Station, and extends from this old-world country town westward over hill, dale and broad woodland to Chorley Wood's breezy common, where it is flanked by trim plantations that provide a perpetual feast for the eye.

SINCE the last issue of this handbook the new extension to Croxley Green & Watford, begun at the latter end of 1922, was completed and opened for traffic on November 2nd, 1925. The new line is only 2½ miles long, but it cost approximately £300,000, owing to the fact that the first mile and a half was practically all in cutting, while the embankment work required was very heavy and no fewer than ten bridges had also to be built. The high bridge over the River Gade gave considerable trouble owing to the presence of springs in the chalk embankments, which necessitated massive monolith piers and extensive pile-driving. The line has been laid out, as the provision of the spacious Goods Yard and Sidings at Croxley Green indicates, with a view to and faith in the future. The station at Watford is architecturally one of the most attractive that has been put up by any railway company in the neighbourhood of London.

This Watford extension is a joint undertaking of the Metropolitan and the London & North Eastern Companies

1926: Struggling for success at Watford and elsewhere

The 1926 calendar, prepared by Raphael Tuck & Son, was used to drive home the message that the Met had arrived in Watford, but not alas at Watford Market Place, the subject of its coloured drawing, or indeed anywhere near the town centre. There was further emphasis on Watford in a folded broadsheet entitled *Watford Homesteads served by the Metro* which included details of the activities of W. Judge and Sons (detached houses), W. E. Bennett & Co (semis with three to four bedrooms, some with garage, at £1,000 upwards) and Watford Ideal Homes Ltd (detached houses designed by Moore, Smith & Colbeck F&ARIBA at £1095 upwards), all three on the Cassiobury Estate. The last-mentioned were sniffily confident of the superiority of their product:

> WHICH IS YOUR CHOICE? The 'Suburban Villa', a stereotyped mass-produced house in which sickly-looking stucco and sham half timbering make one wonder what is underneath, OR Houses of Character and Distinction designed by Architects and constructed by true craftsmen in good honest brickwork – brickwork that is a pleasure to see.

William King & Sons were busy on the Cassiobury Estate and Charles Brightman was at work on the continuation of Cassiobury Park Avenue (Cassiobury Station Estate), with three- and four-bedroom semis on 30ft wide plots selling at £995 and £1,150. Other firms mentioned were Knightley Estates Ltd (detached houses at £1,075 upwards) and Charles C. Swain (houses and bungalows at £850 upwards).

Yet another 'homestead' for the cover picture of *Metro-land* 1926, with an artist too shy to add his or her name. It is interesting that apart from old cottages, the type of house portrayed on these covers always appears to be one that only a First Class season ticket holder could afford.

Wardle seems to have ensured that almost all the advertising was confined to sites within reasonable reach of the Met's Watford and Croxley Green stations. He was keeping a close eye on progress, reporting to Selbie in March that the area covered by Cassiobury Estates Ltd had 100 completed houses, 20 under construction; in all 1,500 were proposed. Brightman had built 12 on the Station Estate with 52 more under construction and a total of 118 proposed. Clifford & Gough had finished six houses on the Rickmansworth Road and eight were under construction with a total of 66 proposed.

On 5 July Wardle informed Selbie that progress in passenger bookings 'is not as good as we desire' but the route was 'becoming more popular'. In the first six months of 1926, bookings to and from Watford (including the Rickmansworth shuttle and Marylebone services) had averaged 14,919 a month (plus 255 season tickets). At Croxley Green, the corresponding figures were 5,390 and 71 seasons. This report also mentions the operation of a through train from Watford to New Cross to convey football supporters to the Millwall *v.* Watford match on Good Friday 1926 with another in the reverse direction for the return match on Easter Monday. Some 3,000 soccer fans had been carried on both days. Wardle also reported delivery to Watford of 500 tons of Staveley slag for road-making near the station.

Fifteen staff handled the new traffic at Watford, seven at Croxley Green; nine were employed on track maintenance and two for freight collection and delivery by road. Selbie and Wedgwood had agreed in 1923–24 on the construction of 16 semi-detached railway staff cottages at a cost of £505 each in Rousebarn Lane, half a mile from the Watford station, this being necessary since, as Selbie bluntly put it, the building that was going on at Watford 'is of houses of a much better class than our men require'.

Metro-land 1926 had a cover depicting yet another upper middle class 'homestead' of the type the Metropolitan hoped to see in greater numbers in Metro-land, especially along the Joint line beyond Rickmansworth. More interested in long distance and freight traffic, the LNER, now the other partner in the Joint line, was generally content to leave active promotion of that line's local passenger business to Baker Street.

Inside, the 1926 edition included a section headed 'Metro-land Railway Developments in 1925' with a map showing Selbie's proposed deep tube relief line between Edgware Road station and Kilburn, designed to eliminate the increasing congestion the growing Metro-land traffic was imposing on the double track between Finchley Road and Baker Street. This proposal was however to come to grief with publication in 1928 of the Ministry of Transport revised version of *Requirements for Passenger Lines*, which made it obligatory to have train doors at both ends of all stock working through deep level tunnels. The Metropolitan could not contemplate costly replacement or rebuilding of most of the coaches used for its Metro-land services to the open saloon design so disliked by its influential longer-distance passengers. Selbie then considered the alternative of larger diameter tunnels with side walkways and cross tunnels to allow for detrainment in emergencies but the Board, finding it all too difficult, deferred a decision. Other ideas were subsequently examined but the solution to the problem had to await the formation of the London Passenger Transport Board in 1933.

Metro-land 1926 also mentioned the 1925 burrowing junction for the Uxbridge line at Harrow, illustrating this with a crude drawing of what looks like a model layout. This work had allowed some improvement in train services to meet the demands imposed by the traffic created by the steadily increasing tempo of new housing construction across Metro-land.

In references to the unhappily beheaded Watford line with its back-street terminus, *Metro-land* claimed that Clark's domestic style station was 'architecturally one of the most attractive that has been put up by any railway company in the neighbourhood of London'. Handsome as it was, his new Metro-land railway architecture of the 1920s and early 1930s would quite soon appear rather unimaginative and ordinary against that of the new suburban Underground stations designed by Charles Holden and his associates.

Preston Road was described as 'still a wayside station' but, 'Its day however is fast coming' and new houses had now been built 'along the country lane that leads to Preston'. Telling Brothers Ltd (later W. A. Telling Ltd), a well known Metro-land firm, advertised their Cuckoo Hill Estate at Pinner.

An aerial photo of part of the Cedars Estate (see below), 'the choicest residential district in Metro-land' revealed its spacious layout at this time. At Chalfont & Latimer, the guide recorded that 'numerous houses and bungalows of tasteful design and moderate cost are being erected'.

'Extensive private building' was noted at Amersham, Chesham, Chesham Bois and Great Missenden, the latter described as a 'small antique township, in a hollow of the Chilterns. Stands extremely high, 400 to 600 feet above sea'. Further out still, at Wendover, 'Considered the most beautiful and picturesque township in the Chilterns. Altitude 450–900 feet', a number of houses were recorded as 'in course of erection in the surrounding district'. Almost all these statements contain a permissible degree of hype but it is interesting that this is a rare if not unique mention in Metro-land publicity of residential development beyond Amersham.

On the Uxbridge line, the Pinn View Estate at Ruislip village was advertised in *Metro-land* for the first time. These houses were somewhat unusual very plain-faced semis with four bedrooms priced at £935 leasehold by Ruislip Manor Ltd and the builder, C. W. Myhill.

Other independent developments advertised in 1926 in the *Evening News* and Metropolitan Railway leaflets and broadsheets may be briefly mentioned. At Harrow, Fidler in Canterbury Road had houses priced at £735–£1,080; on the Marlborough Estate, F. & C. Costin were offering three- to five-bedroom houses from £750 leasehold, £900 freehold upwards, and on Blawith Road, A. V. Lowe advertised three-bedroom semis. At North Harrow, Colrose in Parkside Way had houses 'overlooking the historic Moat Farm', three-bedroom semis with garage space on 30 x 170ft plots, selling at £975 and £990. At Ickenham, Park Road, Treby's two bedroom bungalows on 40 x 200ft plots were priced at £600 and Adams on the Ivy House Estate had houses at the same price. Bungalows were also available at Long Lane, Hillingdon, from F. W. Gapp for £650, also three-bedroom semis for £700.

AERIAL VIEW OF SECTION OF CEDARS ESTATE, RICKMANSWORTH.

1927: Building activity in most parts of Metro-land

The 1927 edition of *Metro-land*, now 112 pages, appeared in mid-year with a very summery cover depicting a middle class picnic party on a steep hillside in typical Chiltern scenery (see opposite).

At Kingsbury Garden Village, more three-bedroom semis are mentioned as being ready for occupation in July, priced at £725 and £775 freehold, many with garage space at the side. The Railway considerably extended its Neasden staff housing in 1926–27, connecting the area with the Garden Village by building Chesham Street to link Village Way and Quainton Street; in both developments the new housing of this period featured pre-fabricated concrete building techniques developed in the 1914–18 war. After the completion of the North Circular Road through the area in 1922, Neasden proceeded rapidly to become a mixed lower middle class/respectable working class between-wars suburb with housing estates erected in quantity either side of the new motor road. The Willesden Council's Nicol Estate on the west side was completed in 1926–27; the large Costain Brentwater Estate on the east side, with its low cost owner-occupier houses, was in progress from the latter year. Next came the large Herbert Glenister Dollis Park Estate of 1928–32, to the south of Costain's and immediately north of the old village centre, these last two estates spreading over the 1893 golf course. A busy shopping centre followed in the early 1930s along Neasden Lane, continuing round the corner at its west end into the North Circular Road. With the 1,872-seat Ritz cinema opened amidst the shops in 1936, the new Neasden was complete. It was later to be unfairly mocked by mid-century satirists and comedians as an archetypal London suburb, but for its first thirty or more years, Neasden was in one sense not typical of Metro-land. Those who came to live here in the new housing of the 1920s and 1930s mostly found employment in the new industrial areas along the North Circular and Edgware Roads, cycling or using buses to get to workplaces; only a minority travelled by Metropolitan trains to central London each day.

Neasden's golf club survived the speculative builders a little longer than the Wembley course. *Metro-land* 1927 mentioned the disappearance of the latter under the advancing tide of the Haymills Barn Hill Estate, coyly not naming names. Anxious to reassure those wondering whether this part of Metro-land had completely lost its open character, the guide's compilers followed up by stating on another page, 'Happily, some forty acres on the upper part of the hill have been acquired by the Wembley Council for a public park.' Things were a little better at Preston Road. The guide records 'many houses are rising on the south side of the line' but comforts the anxious reader by soothingly stating that the country to the north of the line almost as far as Northwick Park & Kenton station 'still remains singularly untouched by the near presence of London'. However, before crossing over the Euston main line, the passenger would now glimpse distant views of activity on the Northwick Estate, with its five-acre Palaestra sports and recreation grounds.

On the Railway's Grange Estate (Grange Gardens) at Pinner, 'Exceptionally Artistic Detached Residences' were announced as nearing completion, These four-bedroom houses were to be sold at £1,600 freehold, £1,400 leasehold. The Metropolitan Railway's architect, C. W. Clark, also designed five detached houses here and elsewhere; seven others were built by the MRCE in 1927–28 and a further 18 by local firms, notably A. V. Evans, who had arrived in Pinner in 1918 and built elsewhere in the area including Mayfield Drive after buying Mayfield House and grounds in 1927.

Metro-land's more distant areas were by no means free of new housing activity at this time. At what the guide called 'the old-fashioned country town of Chesham' there was 'extensive private building on the Lowndes Avenue, Shepherd's Farm and Chartridge Lane Estates'; at Amersham and Chesham Bois, houses were available on the Stanley Hill, Hyron's Farm and Longfield Drive developments.

'Active development' was reported on the Harefield Place and Willowbank Estates near Uxbridge, the former about a mile north of Uxbridge town centre, situated in 'over 700 acres of delightfully wooded countryside' and illustrated by a single new and empty house looking rather lost in it. Willowbank, on the outermost north western edge of the town, sited between the Grand Union Canal and the River Colne, seemed likely to be a good choice for anglers.

Along the Uxbridge line, the MRCE opened four more estates in 1927: Hillingdon Mount (7.25 acres); Eastcote Hill (10.75 acres); Manor Farm, Eastcote Road, Ruislip (19.5 acres); and Elm Grove, Ruislip (21.5 acres). Manor Farm was advertised in the 1927 *Metro-land*, offering single plots with a minimum size of 30 x 180ft. Also available were 'large sections' for development by builders.

The Hillingdon Mount Estate, with its frontage to Long Lane, north of the Railway, had a background which throws some light on the relationships between the MRCE and its parent. This site had been purchased by the Railway Company in September 1922 for £1,065, the intention being to use it for a freight yard adjacent to the proposed Hillingdon station. However, as explained earlier, negotiations with the developers for that station yielded a gift of land to provide a goods yard at the Uxbridge end of the proposed station. This allowed the Railway Company to sell the Long Lane land to the MRCE for what was to become known as the Hillingdon Mount Estate, the MRCE paying the Railway Company £1,117 and then spending £2,050 on road-making and services for 20 house plots and making tennis courts, a total of £3,167. The realisation from the sale of the house plots was £4,600 leaving the MRCE a net profit of £1,433.

New independent developments advertised in the 1927 edition included Comben & Wakeling's St Augustine's Estate, south of Preston Road station, 'planned and developed on the best Garden Suburb lines with semi-detached houses to suit all tastes and requirements – crowding and close repetition are avoided' (much the same description as used in 1926 for the firm's Park Lane Estate). Prices here for three-bedroom houses ranged from £825 to £1,000, four bedrooms £1,100 to £1,450. At Ruislip, the Church Croft Estate (Croft Gardens, Mid Croft, South Drive) was announced.

Other new developments advertised in 1927 in the *Evening News* and elsewhere should be mentioned. A large estate by T. F. Nash Ltd at Kenton, the first of this firm's projects, begun in 1925 and now well under way was sited just north east of the LMSR station but was also within reach of Northwick Park & Kenton, half to one mile to the south west and thus can be regarded as within Metro-land. Houses here with garage space were selling at £850 upwards. By December 1928, a total of 740 had been erected with 680 occupied; by 1931 some 2,200 houses were built as well as a shopping parade in Kenton Road, with two floors of residential accommodation above.

At Chesham, bungalows in Bellingdon Road on the Chesham Hills Estate were priced as low as £600. Ruislip's Windmill Estate (The Grange), had detached bungalows and houses at £675 and £875.

Two other publications at this time call for notice. Wardle's office produced 10,000 copies of a folder, *Watford's New Facility*, with maps showing details of the Metropolitan Railway bus service begun on 2 November 1927 between its station and Watford town centre. This was distributed to Watford residents and passengers using the station. *London's Pleasureland Cheap fare and Pleasure Party Arrangements on The Metro*, issued free of charge in the spring, directed attention to the country districts served and the facilities for pleasure parties and walking tours.

IF you are seeking a home—large or small, old-world or modern—you will readily find it in Metro-land, the glorious countryside, easily and quickly reached by the Metropolitan Railway.

Nowhere in or around London is there a district that possesses so many sterling advantages, nor a residential area that so closely approaches the ideal. The train service is frequent and fast, the Season Ticket rates are low, the Educational facilities are excellent and the local Golf courses both numerous and good.

BAKER ST. STATION, N.W.1.

Send coupon below to the Company's Commercial Manager, Baker Street Station, N.W.1, and secure copy of House-seeker's Guide, which sets out in concise form the manifold housing propositions obtaining in Metro-land.

Commercial Manager,
Metropolitan Railway,
Baker Street Station, N.W.1.
Please send post free copy of The Metro. House-seeker's guide.

Name.....................................

Address..................................

R. H. SELBIE, General Manager.

An advertisement in *The Railway Magazine* December 1927, an issue which contains a main article on Baker Street station and its traffic by J F Gairns.

Cottages at Latimer on the cover of Metro-land 1928. The white strip is not a printing fault: Lord Chesham had ordered wooden boards to be placed across the railing spikes after a favourite dog of his had been killed when jumping over this fence. The boards were still in place in 2006.

1928: More houses for Metro-land and a puff for Ruislip

The cover of the 166-page 1928 *Metro-land* featured a coloured photo of cottages at Latimer village, set amongst woods about one mile north of the Metropolitan Railway station at Chalfont & Latimer. This remains an unspoilt part of Metro-land today. Inside, the formula was much as before, with some repetition of text from earlier issues. Ruislip, no longer described as a village but as a 'little township', was said to be 'growing rapidly in all directions'. In the description of Pinner, a note of conscience may be detected in the writer's comment on the recent destruction of elm trees to make way for new houses: '. . . those who lay out building estates ought to spare every fine tree they can'.

Fearing the reader might be put off Northwood by what was visible from the railway the writer is careful to say, 'the other Northwood, which is not so well seen from the train, is a place of charming villas, large and small ...' A 'new and particularly pleasing suburb of Northwood' is recorded as 'being laid out on the rising ground which leads by Copse Wood on the road to Ruislip' (this was the Copse Wood Estate, building over yet another piece of rural Metro-land).

The new Eastcote Hill MRCE estate, alongside the Railway on its north side, was now under way, with plots from £5 per foot frontage and houses 'now ready' for £995. Also available here were shop plots on the main road from £10 per foot frontage – another Metro-land suburb was appearing. Elm Grove MRCE Estate, south of Ruislip station, would soon be offering plots with 50ft frontage at prices from £4 a foot, for the erection of small houses and bungalows. At another MRCE development, Hillingdon Mount, prices for plots started at £4 per foot frontage. At Rickmansworth, the MRCE were opening up a new section of the Cedars Estate, close to the station, with plots of 50 x 150ft priced from £200 each. By December 1928, 188 houses had been erected on the Cedars and Moneyhill Estates, of which 184 were occupied, but 486 acres were still available for development.

An advertisement under the heading 'Metropolitan Railway' revealed a new development on surplus land bought many years before: the Sherrick Green Estate, on the north side of the line between Willesden Green and Dollis Hill stations. As the freeholder, the Railway Company built roads, laid services and arranged building leases, taking profit in the form of ground rents. With two roads completed at a cost of £8,430, it was reported to the Board that the associated ground rents would yield £1,500 or 7½ per cent on outlay. *Metro-land* announced 'Houses ... with varying and pleasing elevations and of sound construction' all with 99 years' lease at purchase prices of £795 upwards.

New independent developments mentioned or advertised in this edition were: the Toley, South Forty Farm and Bateman Building Co. estates at Preston Road; at North Harrow, Northumberland Road, E. S. Reid had built detached and semi-detached houses selling at £950–£1,600 (see right), and at Watford, new developments were in The Chase, Maythorne Close, Whippendell Road, King George's Avenue and Kelmscott Crescent.

Publications from Wardle's office in 1928 included *A Day in the Country*, containing details of the countryside reached by the railway, with information on cheap fares and catering facilities.

There was also a booklet called *Ruislip – London's Healthiest Suburb*, making a second use of the attractive coloured cover of the 1926 *Metro-land*. In the introductory text the anonymous copywriter worked hard to press home the advantages of Ruislip. There were now 117 trains daily, covering the 13.25 miles from Baker Street in 25 minutes, less time than it took to read the evening paper. Carried away by enthusiasm, the scribe declared Ruislip the 'least spoiled of the residential districts round London', with green fields on all sides and 'health-giving woods' close at hand:

> . . . there is a 'something' about the district that is irresistible. It may be its assurance of charm, the freshness of its air, or its settled look of ancient peace. Whatever it be, it suggests a new standard of home life; it confirms your sudden conviction that this is the place of your desire.

Local details and photographs, a summary of local history, a list of season ticket rates and fares followed this laudatory introduction. Enclosed with the booklet was a loose broadsheet advertising schools, local businesses, shops, and houses and plots currently available. This last featured advertisements for: Manor Farm; Church

Two pages from the 1928 Ruislip booklet mentioned in the text.

WHAT IS RUISLIP?

RUISLIP claims to be the most accessible and the least spoiled of the residential districts around London. It can be reached in less time than it takes to read your Evening Paper, and it has just that quiet reserve with just that degree of friendliness which will make you want to live there for always. If you have been hesitating where to make your home, you need hesitate no more.

On all sides of Ruislip are green fields; close at hand are health-giving woods. There is a good train service; a Golf Course lies at your very door; you will find houses ready to live in which are reasonable in cost, or land for building a house to your own individual taste. In a word, nothing is lacking that is required to make the perfect residential district.

Moreover, apart from the definite attractions of Ruislip there is a "something" about the district that is irresistible. It may be its assurance of charm, the freshness of its air, or its settled look of ancient peace. Whatever it be, it suggests a new standard of home life; it confirms your sudden conviction that this is the place of your desire.

Ruislip spells Health and Home

Page Three

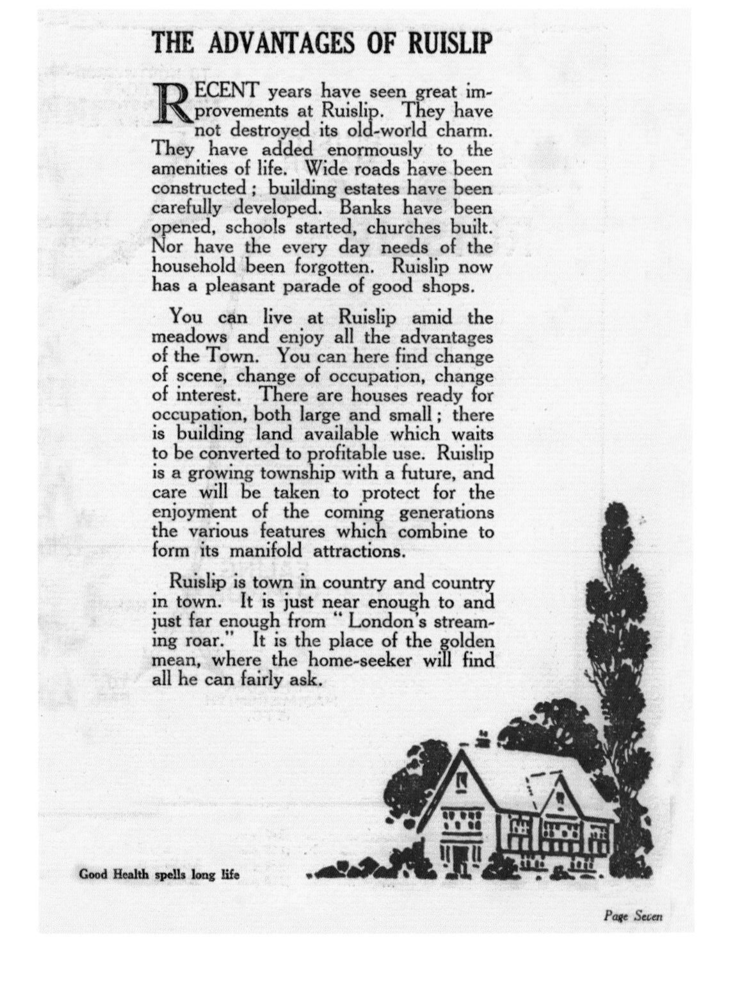

THE ADVANTAGES OF RUISLIP

RECENT years have seen great improvements at Ruislip. They have not destroyed its old-world charm. They have added enormously to the amenities of life. Wide roads have been constructed; building estates have been carefully developed. Banks have been opened, schools started, churches built. Nor have the every day needs of the household been forgotten. Ruislip now has a pleasant parade of good shops.

You can live at Ruislip amid the meadows and enjoy all the advantages of the Town. You can here find change of scene, change of occupation, change of interest. There are houses ready for occupation, both large and small; there is building land available which waits to be converted to profitable use. Ruislip is a growing township with a future, and care will be taken to protect for the enjoyment of the coming generations the various features which combine to form its manifold attractions.

Ruislip is town in country and country in town. It is just near enough to and just far enough from "London's streaming roar." It is the place of the golden mean, where the home-seeker will find all he can fairly ask.

Good Health spells long life

Page Seven

Croft; Windmill Hill; Poplars Close; St Catherine's, Bury Street; Manor View, Eastcote Road; and the domain of Ruislip Manor Ltd. House prices quoted range from £960 to £1,390. By the end of 1928, 317 new houses had been erected on the post-war Ruislip area estates, with 26 more under construction towards a total of 789 proposed.

The 1928 Metro-land developments advertised in the *Evening News* and elsewhere offered some variety of price and location and may be summarised as follows:

Harrow: Parkside Estate, Whitmoor Road, Burdett (Harrow) Ltd, £1,150–£1,600, backing onto park with 3–4 bedrooms and oak parquet floors; Lerwick, Rusland and Torver Roads, Messrs Lambert, £860.

Kenton: facing station, Central Estates Company, £795–£1,275; Westfield Estate, Ebrington Road, Edwards, £850 upwards; Woodhill Crescent, Geo. H. Gillett & Co., £1,050.

Pinner: Parkfield Estate (Park Avenue), Sidney Sharp, three-bedroom semis £760–£985.

Ickenham: Ivy House Farm Estate, Arohead Ltd, £715.

Ruislip: Windmill Hill Estate, W. G. Carter, unusually offering rent of new three-bedroom houses at £90 a year, four-bedroom type at £129.

Rickmansworth: Money Hill Park, large semis, £1,050.

The map from the 1928 Ruislip booklet. Note how the junction at Rayners Lane has been brought closer to Ruislip Manor to deceive the eye of the reader.

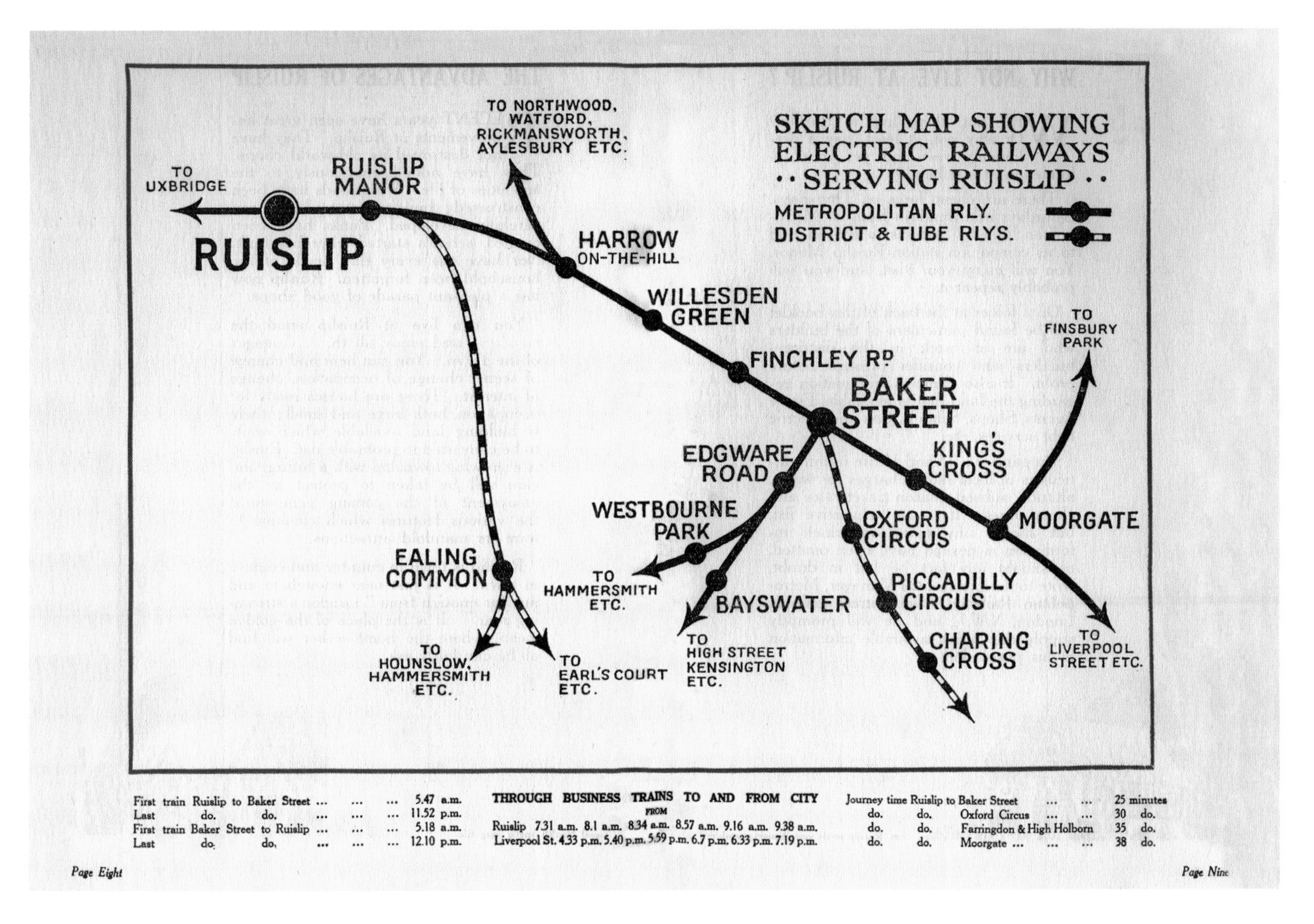

A 1930 photograph of Chiltern Court, the extensive block of apartments, restaurant, function hall etc. which was completed from first floor level upwards above Baker Street station in 1929 to the designs of the Company's architect, Charles Walter Clark FRIBA.

1929: Chiltern Court, plans for Rayners Lane & more Metro-land suburbia

Despite the growing pace of suburban expansion and the commercial need to encourage it, the quiet, relaxing attractions of the Railway's outer reaches were not neglected by Wardle's department and a nostalgic rural theme was chosen for the cover of the 128-page *Metro-land* published in 1929. Boldly executed in strong colours, with deep shadows and lit by a low shaft of sunlight, the picture of an old timber-framed cottage was one of the best covers in the whole series. The artist was Michael Reilly, who also worked for the Great Western Railway in the 1930s.

A new feature in this edition was *The Story of Chiltern Court*. This large mansard-roofed block of apartments with its 250-seat restaurant, cinema and shops was designed by Charles Walter Clark, FRIBA, to occupy the air space over Baker Street station. Although referring back to Edwardian commercial architecture, it was successful in boosting the Company's public image. Tenants began to move in at the end of 1929 and the restaurant was opened on 15 November.

This edition also made the first mention of a major new residential development at Rayners Lane, described as 'the loneliest station on the Metropolitan Railway, apparently unfriended, unvisited and untrod'. The 1906 halt was certainly not very busy until this time but it did serve an isolation hospital, a rifle range, two sewage farms and a few scattered cottages as well as providing an interchange facility

FRESH AND REFRESHING

FRESH and refreshing aptly describes the Reid house and its proven superiority is reflected in the fact that nearly one hundred have been built within the past year; that many have been bought before they were erected and that an even greater number have been sold through the recommendation of satisfied purchasers.

With a Reid house goes a pledge of quality and after sale service. They embrace features usually only to be found in more expensive houses, whilst the excellence of the materials used and workmanship employed will be readily recognised by discriminating house-seekers.

The houses illustrated above represent but a few of a wide range of types available and designs to meet individual requirements can be readily arranged at the minimum of cost. The purchase prices range from £895 to £1,600 freehold, and by payment of a small sum possession can be secured; the balance being spread over a period of years.

The Reid house represents an honest endeavour to produce a house that will give lasting pride to the purchaser and critical inspection at all or any stage of construction is cordially invited.

Why not write or call to-day, or phone Harrow 0712, for further particulars? You will not be worried to buy.

E.S.REID ESTATE OFFICES

NORTH·HARROW·STATION & HARROW·GARDEN·VILLAGE, M^{DX}

SAY YOU SAW IT IN "METRO-LAND."

Page 108

SAY YOU SAW IT IN "METRO-LAND."

Page 109

Advertisements in the 1929 *Metro-land*

between Metropolitan and District services; there were lonelier halts and stations north of Aylesbury. Be that as it may, the *Metro-land* copywriter declared the halt's day had come, since it would now serve as the station for 'Harrow Garden Village', to be built mostly north of the line, across an area of open country on which 'the architects had been 'able to create at leisure'. Here, on 211 acres, some 1,000 houses and 240 shops were planned for a layout featuring 'wide avenues, generous circles, closes and open spaces, good garden plots, tennis courts and recreation grounds'. Sites were to be reserved for churches and schools.

Initially only 187 acres had been bought by the MRCE for £50,000 in 1928, using money advanced by the railway company at 4 per cent interest, the capital repayable within five years on the grounds that the project would 'bring valuable traffic and other advantages to the Metropolitan Railway'. A further loan of £30,000 was promised after three years if development was by then well advanced, providing a proper security. In the advertising pages of the 1929 *Metro-land*, E. S. Reid was the first builder to announce a stake in this new suburb (see above). Reid was a former Deputy Engineer for Harrow Council but had resigned in 1928 to begin his housebuilding activities in Northumberland Road, close to the railway at North Harrow.

For all available

HOUSES, FLATS, SHOPS & LAND

IN

KINGSBURY
WEMBLEY PARK
PRESTON ROAD
KENTON, HARROW
WEALDSTONE
HARROW WEALD
HATCH END, PINNER

apply to

Head Office: 132, KENTON ROAD, KENTON,
Telephone: Harrow 0994.

Branch Offices:	*Phone:*
HARROW & WEALDSTONE STATION	Harrow 0773
WEMBLEY PARK	Wembley 1707
PRESTON ROAD	Wembley 2496
HATCH END	Hatch End 149

Selected list of suitable properties promptly forwarded free of charge.

SAY YOU SAW IT IN "METRO-LAND."

Page 110

GILLETT'S *DISTINCTIVE* HOUSES

Reasonable in cost yet vastly superior to many offered at a higher price, Gillett's houses, happily placed on Kenton's highest point, will undoubtedly appeal. They are built up to a standard and not down to a price; they represent the successful outcome of a keen endeavour to satisfy every need, and everything likely to lessen labour and increase home comfort will be found in their design.

The prices range from £1,045 to £1,525 and only superior materials and conscientious workmanship have been employed. Each house has a good garden and liberal frontage; each house a spacious garage or room for one. Their situation is both exclusive and accessible, and on the estate is a splendid club house with 22 tennis courts, whilst an 18-hole golf course adjoins the station.

Why not write, 'phone or call to-day for a copy of our "Houses of distinction" booklet describing the houses in detail—it will be well worth your while.

GEO. H. GILLETT & Co. Ltd.
Telephone - Harrow 2514.
WOODCOCK HILL LANE, KENTON, HARROW

SAY YOU SAW IT IN "METRO-LAND."

Page 111

Further out, this edition now reported housebuilding in the very heart of rural Metro-land. Around the 'most beautiful neighbourhood' of Chalfont & Latimer residential construction was in progress close to the station, also on the Nightingale, Pollards Park, Beechwood and Old House Farm Estates. At Chesham, 60 houses had already been erected on the Chiltern Hills Estate, a name which surely caused a shiver of despair among the rambling community. New building was proceeding in Devonshire Avenue, a few minutes' walk north of Amersham station.

Nearer London, Cutlers were busy reinforcing their dominance in the claylands of North Harrow, advertising their cheapest 'semi-detached brick-built villas 'with room for garage on the Highfield and Ridgeway Estates at £885 freehold. After paying £45 deposit, purchasers repaid the balance at £1 8s 2d a week. These Cutler houses were quite well built but their dull uniformity, reinforced by the regular building lines along the grid type road layout, was relieved only by the roses cultivated in the clay of their front gardens and the twee pictures of cottages, windmills, galleons and other subjects in the coloured glass leaded lights of their front doors and landing windows. This feature, once a typical characteristic of this part of Metro-land has now almost, if not completely, disappeared as a result of subsequent reglazing.

Somewhat higher in the the social scale, at Northwood, was the Gatehill Estate of Harry Neal Ltd, eight minutes' walk from the station. This was on a site sloping 'gently south west from a height of 400ft.' and each house would be 'built to suit the owner's requirements'. Some moderately large detached houses appeared here from 1924 onwards, the construction materials brought in via the firm's private siding on the Up side, beyond the London end of Northwood station.

A. Robinson was advertising detached and semi-detached houses at Mount View, Rickmansworth, on the section of the Cedars Estate west of the railway, where more houses were to be built to the acre than on the main section, and prices started at £995.

A newcomer on the Northwick Park Estate, within reasonable distance of the Metropolitan station of that name, was Edgar Elliot, who in this edition of the guide was advertising detached houses at £1,000 to £4,000; whilst on the Cuckoo Hill Estate, south of the line and some eight minutes' walk from Pinner station, Telling Bros Ltd announced 'Superior Freehold Villas and Spacious Building Plots' with no price stated.

Apart from these announcements in the 1929 *Metro-land*, other sources yield information on activity at this time. At Parkside Way, North Harrow, Lawson & Wright offered semis at £825 and nearby, in Kingsfield Avenue, A. J. King had three and four-bedroom houses at £960–£1,400. At Pinner, just south of the Railway, the West End Farm Estate was in progress and at the Eastbury Estate, Northwood, three- and four-bedroom semis and detached houses were ready at £1,025 upwards. And on Long Lane, Hillingdon Park Estate, J. F. Langer was offering houses at £795.

Detached houses on offer in the 1929 *Metro-land*.

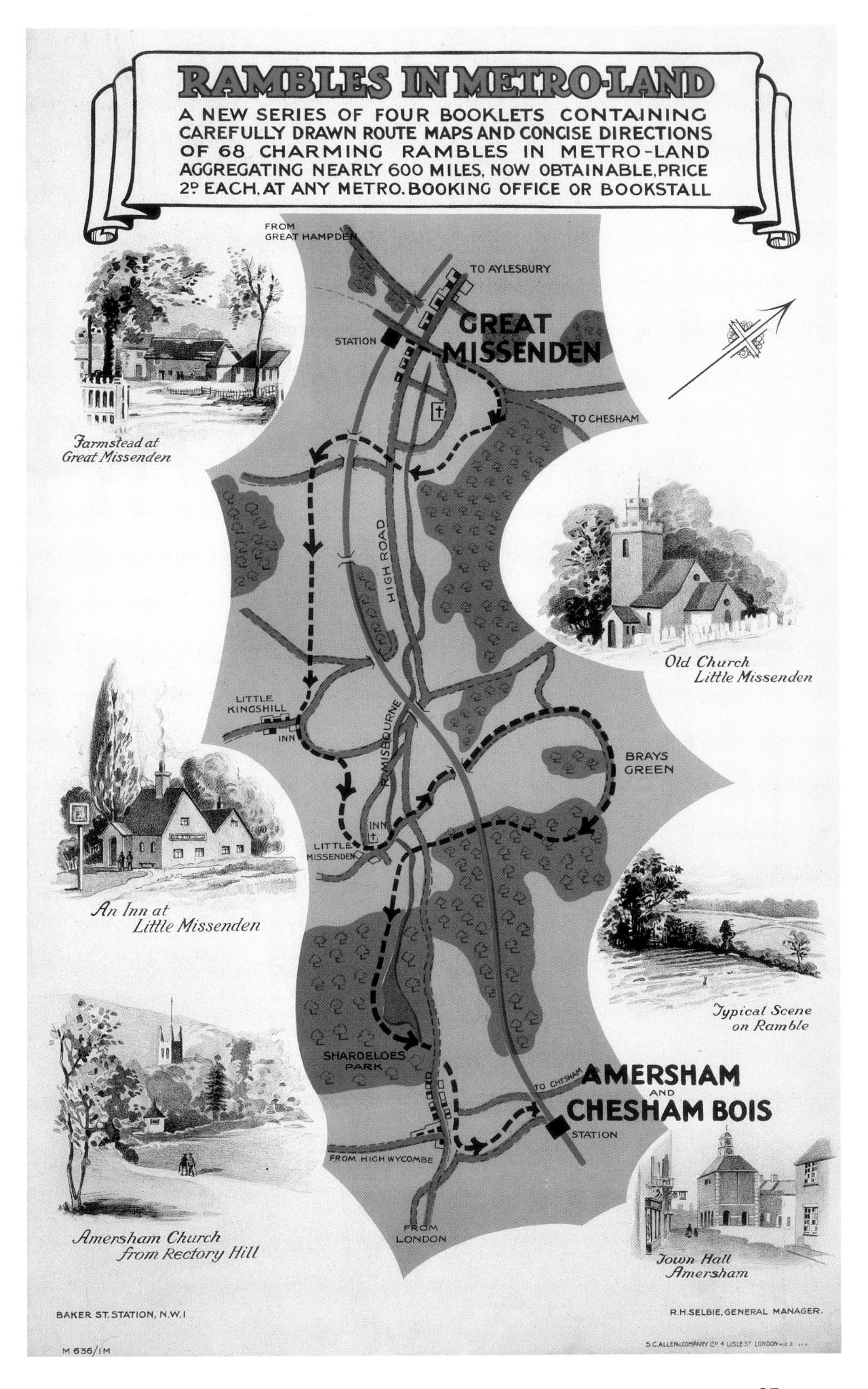

For walkers, a 'New Series' of four Metropolitan Railway booklets (1930/1931) offered guidance for 'nearly 600 miles' of rambling in return for an outlay of eight old pennies, the price of eight issues of a popular daily paper.

1930: The MRCE goes 450ft up at Amersham and ignites growth at Rayners Lane
Another rather splendid cover (above) adorned the 1930 issue of *Metro-land*, depicting Harrow on the Hill at sunset, the old church commanding the summit and below, a stately row of elms. Sadly these fine trees, once such a feature of Middlesex, are now long gone, victims of virulent disease.

Free publicity material on offer in *The Railway Yearbook*, 1930.

METRO-LAND FOR HEALTH

HAVE you ever realised the joy of living in the country; the pleasure of rural surroundings and bracing air? Have you ever thought of the definite advantages to be gained; the economies to be effected; the new view point that a change of scene, occupation and interest will undoubtedly bring?

In Metro-land—London's nearest countryside—you will find all that you can reasonably ask. It has character and charm; variety and interest. It is the most accessible and least spoiled residential district around London, and its train service is the envy of all. There are through trains to and from the City both morning and evening; there are "non-stop" trains, "cheap" trains, "theatre" trains—everything in fact that you can possibly desire.

But this is not all. Metro-land lays definite claim to be the most healthy district around London. The climate is mild and equable; the air is clean and invigorating and the subsoil, for the most part, is gravel. There are unlimited facilities for outdoor recreation; there are fifteen golf courses from which to choose; educational and shopping facilities are exceptionally liberal, whilst the Season Ticket rates will be found within the reach of all.

In Metro-land there are neat little villas standing in their own trim gardens; stately mansions surrounded by park-like grounds, and there is also a multitude of out-of-the-way nooks and corners where the life of the country goes on serene, unspoilt by the changes that have overwhelmed the countryside elsewhere.

It will pay you to consider carefully the many advantages of living in Metro-land and to review the active housing development that is taking place in all directions. To help you in this connection, a profusely illustrated Handbook has been prepared containing a varied selection of exclusive designs and plans of charming houses, and also a "Broadsheet" that sets out in detail the various housing propositions obtaining in Metro-land.

The coupon below will bring you a free copy of each, by return.

Commercial Manager,
Metropolitan Railway,
Baker St. Station, London, N.W. 1.

Please send, post free, copy of "Where to Live" Handbook and also House-Seekers Broadsheet.

Name..........

Address..........

....

BAKER ST. STATION, N.W.1. R. H. SELBIE, *General Manager*

A preliminary announcement ('new roads will shortly be made . . .') anticipated the Weller Estate at Amersham, the MRCE's latest and final venture under the control of the Metropolitan Railway. Purchased in 1930, the 78 acres north and south of the railway included Woodside Farm, built in 1670 by Mary Pennington and of historical interest for its associations with Oliver Cromwell and William Penn. Here 535 mainly

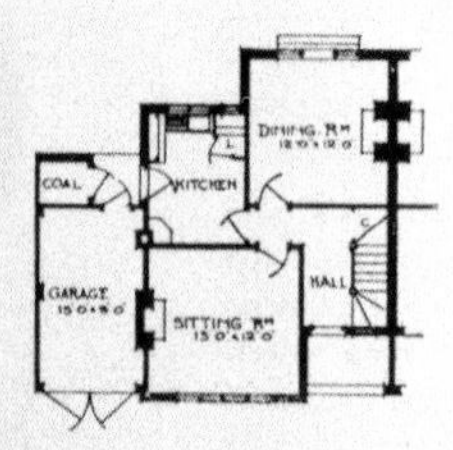

TYPE "A"

These attractive Semi-Detached Houses, each standing in a plot with frontage of 35 feet and a depth of about 125 feet have been erected in Woodside Close, facing a permanent open space and within 3 minutes' walk of station and a minute of the shops. Also in the corner of the Close and south of Railway fronting the Drive.

The properties are constructed in brick with red tile roof, white shingled elevation and oak half timbering.

There is a Built-in Garage with a covered way Coal Store. Tiled Kitchen. Leaded Glass Windows in Crittall Frames, Wired for Electric Light and ample number of Power and Gas Points. Tiled Bathroom with enclosed bath. Main Drainage.

An enlarged "A" type is also available in Woodside Close with the kitchen extended in line with the Dining Room rear wall and thereby also enlarging the first floor third Bedroom, the price being £900 Freehold.

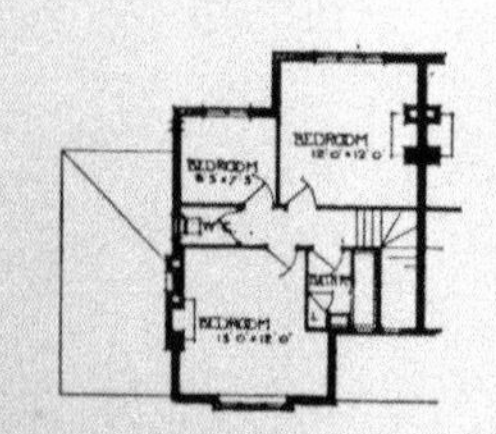

£875 FREEHOLD

TOTAL DEPOSIT £25

NO ROAD CHARGES

NO STAMP DUTIES

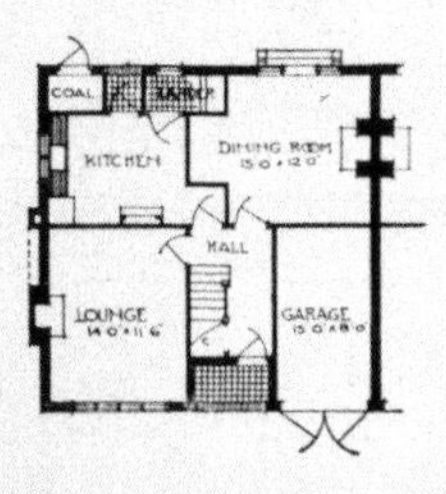

TYPE "B"

An exceptionally well planned 4 Bedroom Semi-Detached House with a built-in Garage. Constructed in brick with rough cast spar elevation and red tile roof, and having oak half timbering to the overhanging bay to first floor with red tiles under.

These properties have been erected in plots well set back from the Road in the corner of Woodside Close, conveniently situated within 3 minutes' walk of the Station and Shops, and facing a permanent open space.

This house could be repeated in The Drive, south of the Railway, on a plot with 33 feet frontage and a depth of about 130 feet at same price.

All the modern features are found in these houses. Tiled Bathroom, with enclosed bath, and Kitchen, leaded glass windows. Dwarf Brick Wall with posts and chains and chain link side fencing. Main Drainage.

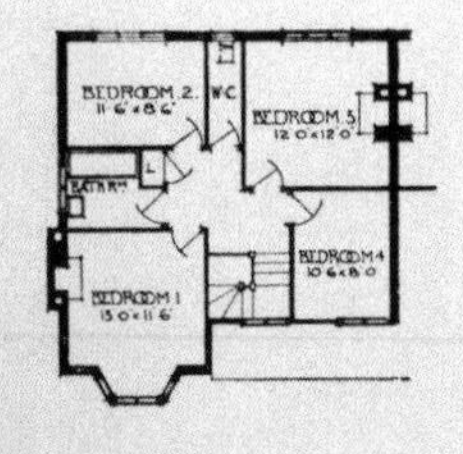

£985 FREEHOLD

TOTAL DEPOSIT £25

NO ROAD CHARGES

NO STAMP DUTIES

Four pages from the 1930 launch booklet for the MRCE Weller Estate, located on either side of the railway at Amersham station between Grimsdell's Lane and Stanley Avenue.

semi-detached houses priced at £875 upwards and 51 shops were proposed. Concerned about the commercial prospects of an estate so far from London, the MRCE asked the Met board for subsidies for each house or shop built, only to meet with refusal on the grounds that such financial help might cause problems with the other member of the Metropolitan & Great Central Joint Committee. The Metropolitan Board also nursed doubts about the validity of the precedent subsidy given to the Wembley Park Estate Company in 1914–27.

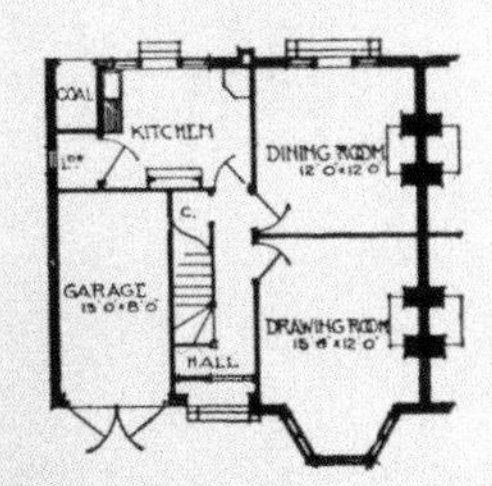

TYPE "C"

A larger 3 Bedroom Semi-Detached House constructed in brick with brown shingled elevations, a red tile roof and deep bay windows under an oak timbered Gable. Frontage of plot 32 feet and depth of about 125 feet.

These houses have been erected and are delightfully situated in Woodside Close within 3 minutes' walk of Station and Shops and facing a permanent open space, and also in the corner of the Close well set back from the Road and on plots widening at the rear but with less frontage.

Each property has a built-in Garage, Tiled Bathroom, with enclosed bath. Tiled Kitchen, fitted with hot water boiler and "Easywork" type of dresser. Electric Light, with liberal number of power and gas points. Leaded Glass Windows in Crittall Frames. Main Drainage.

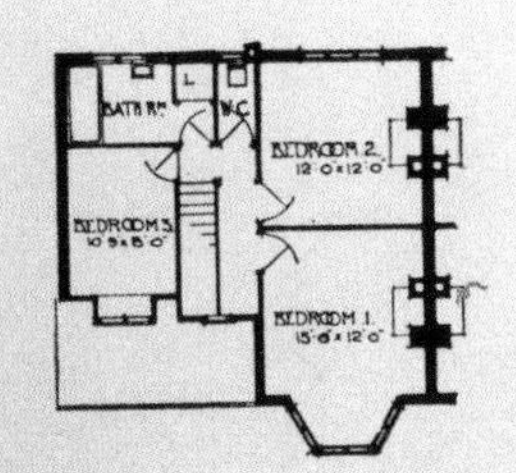

£895 FREEHOLD

TOTAL DEPOSIT £25

NO ROAD CHARGES

NO STAMP DUTIES

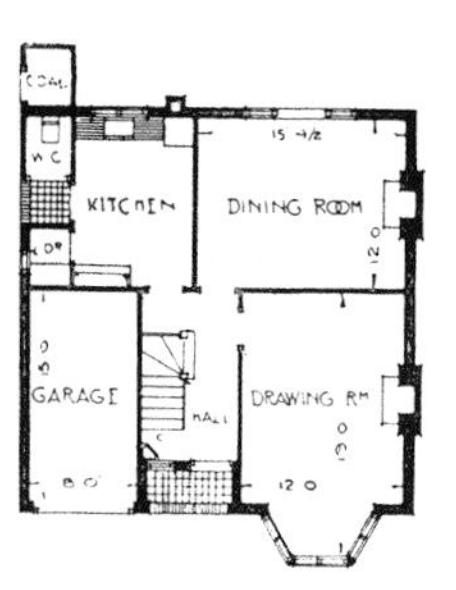

TYPE "D"

An imposing Detached Residence in The Rise, on that undulating part of the Estate south of railway, within 3 minutes' walk of Station and Shops. The site which has a frontage of 35 ft. and a depth of about 200 ft. was specially selected in order to give beautiful views of Chiltern Countryside, the surrounding woods and old Amersham.

The property is substantially constructed in brick and white cement elevations, with red tile roof and oak half timbering above and hanging tiles between the bay windows.

The accommodation comprises 4 good size Bedrooms, Tiled Bathroom with enclosed bath and pedestal lavatory basin, separate W.C., Drawing Room, Dining Room, Tiled Kitchen with hot water boiler and cabinet dresser, outside W.C., Wash Basin under stairs in hall, Built-in Garage, etc. Glass tiles in roof above hall. Main Drainage.

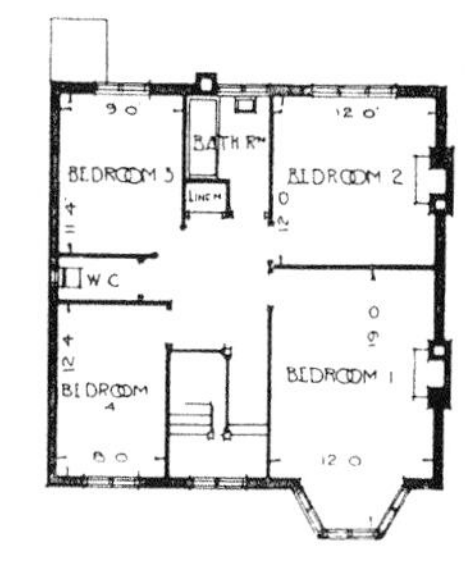

£1200 FREEHOLD

TOTAL DEPOSIT £25

NO ROAD CHARGES

NO STAMP DUTIES

To reinforce interest, a booklet about the Weller Estate was quickly rushed out, so quickly indeed that it had to be illustrated throughout with coloured drawings rather than photographs. Four types of house at prices from £875 to £1,200 were shown and described, supported with a plan of the area, details of purchase arrangements and local information. The estate was described as 'adjacent to the station near the Common and Chesham Bois and within a mile of the old town of Amersham with its old Georgian buildings and quaint old inns and courtyards'.

Harrow Garden Village and Rayners Lane station, as depicted in the 1931 edition of *Metro-land*.

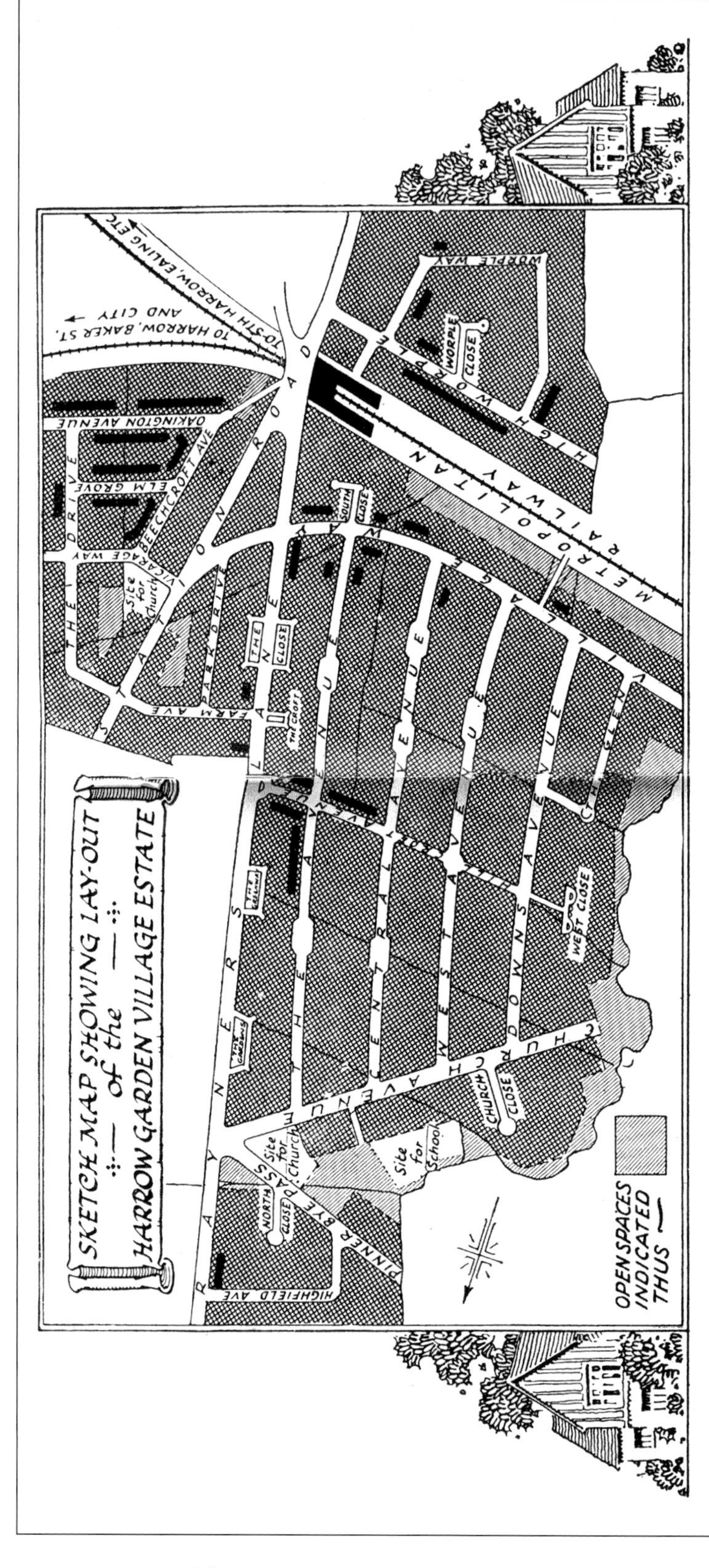

HARROW GARDEN VILLAGE ESTATE
SKETCH MAP SHOWING LAY-OUT of the HARROW GARDEN VILLAGE ESTATE
OPEN SPACES INDICATED THUS —
RAYNERS LANE
METROPOLITAN RAILWAY
TO STH HARROW, EALING ETC.
TO HARROW, BAKER ST. AND CITY
OAKINGTON AVENUE
ELM GROVE
BEECHCROFT AVE
THE DRIVE
VICARAGE WAY
FARM AVE
WORPLE WAY
WORPLE CLOSE
THE CLOSE
THE CROFT
SOUTH CLOSE
CENTRAL AVENUE
WEST AVENUE
DOWNS AVENUE
CHURCH AVENUE
CHURCH CLOSE
WEST CLOSE
NORTH CLOSE
Site for Church
Site for School
HIGHFIELD AVE
THIS beautifully laid out and well timbered Estate of over 213 acres, with 16 acres of permanent open spaces, recreation grounds and tennis courts, adjoins Rayners Lane Station, and is within 11 miles of Baker Street, which is served by over 200 trains daily, and a mile from Pinner and 1½ miles from Harrow.
The construction of some five miles of Roads has nearly been completed, and over 20,000 feet frontage has already been disposed of.
Freehold Building Sites, in small or large sections, are now available at the price from £5 per foot frontage, for the erection of Detached or Semi-detached Houses and for Shops, Business Premises, Banking, Cinema, Hotel, etc., from £20 per foot frontage. Houses for Sale and Shops to be Let or for Sale.
For further particulars and plan, apply :—
H. GIBSON, The Metropolitan Railway Country Estates Ltd.,
Baker Street Station, N.W.1. Welbeck—6688.

There was more confidence about 'Harrow Garden Village' at Rayners Lane, where the guide noted that the first residents had 'already taken up their abode'. All pretence was now thrown aside as readers were no longer invited to explore the charming unspoilt countryside of this corner of Metro-land, but rather to view its spoiling:

> Those who are interested in the rise of a township from its very first beginnings can here watch the rising walls of what has every promise of developing into a popular and pleasant suburb.

It was indeed to prove highly successful. Offering in the main the popular and affordable three-bedroom semi under £1,000, its completion would coincide with the London suburban housing boom, which after 1932, saw a rapid recovery from the economic depression with output of private sector houses around London rising steeply to reach a between-wars peak in 1934. By the end of 1932, 376 houses and 29 shops had been erected at Rayners Lane by eight building firms.

Early in the lead was E. S. Reid, who lived on the site in one of his own houses on what became Oakington Avenue. Finding that existing local roads could not cope with the weight and frequency of deliveries of building materials, Reid paid the Metropolitan £1,000 for a private siding. His houses (see below), at £895 to £1,350, were advertised across four pages of the 1930 *Metro-land* but the more expensive ones proved difficult to sell quickly in this location. A. Robinson, also building houses here in 'seven artistic types' from £850 to £1,150, would also let them to 'approved tenants' from £65 a year, 'Early application essential to avoid disappointment'. In his *Metro-land* advert, Robinson mentioned the 16 acres reserved for open spaces and sports in what he described as 'Undoubtedly the Estate of the future'.

A GOOD MOVE

— TO HARROW GARDEN VILLAGE

21 MINUTES FROM BAKER STREET.
HOUSES OF VARYING TYPE
BUILT BY WELL-KNOWN BUILDERS
AVAILABLE AT POPULAR PRICES.
LIBERAL OPEN SPACES, TENNIS COURTS, ETC.
EXCELLENT SITES FOR HOUSES AND SHOP PLOTS
IN COMMANDING POSITIONS. FULL PARTICULARS
FROM H. GIBSON, GENERAL OFFICES, BAKER S.T STATION
CHEAP TICKETS FROM ALL METRO. STATIONS
ON THURSDAYS, SATURDAYS AND SUNDAYS TO
RAYNERS LANE (FOR HARROW GARDEN VILLAGE) ADJOINING ESTATE

A Metropolitan Railway poster for Harrow Garden Village.

HARROW GARDEN VILLAGE ESTATE

Type "A" House. *See Page 116 for Particulars of Price, etc.*

Type "C" House. *See Page 117 for Particulars of Price, etc.*

NOWHERE in the whole perimeter of London has more remarkable development taken place during the past year than at Harrow Garden Village and, similarly, nowhere in or around London, can better value be obtained than that afforded by the various types of Reid Houses which form the outstanding feature of this increasingly popular Estate.
Reid houses are built to give lasting pleasure and pride; they are selling as fast as they are built; they are recommended by purchasers, surveyors and Building Societies; they reflect consummate care and thoroughness of workmanship and at every stage of their construction the closest scrutiny is cordially welcomed for the more thoroughly they are examined, the more apparent will become the value offered.
With a Reid house there is no such thing as monotony for they are so varied as to preserve the individuality of each and all. Again, with a Reid house goes a definite pledge of quality, satisfaction and after-sale service, whilst, behind it all, there is a friendly personal factor, a keenness to help and an assurance of a "square-deal" in every detail.

E.S. REID, STATION ESTATE OFFICE

HARROW GARDEN VILLAGE
RAYNERS LANE STATION, MIDDSX
TELEPHONE: PINNER 987

Page 114 Page 115

The grand interior of Chiltern Court Restaurant. The restaurant contractors, Spiers & Pond, complained that it was unprofitable because Clark's décor was 'outdated'.

Robinson's publicity also included a reference to his Eastbury Estate at Northwood, 'eight minutes walk from the station' and 'surrounded by woodlands, pastures and peaceful country lanes'. Prices here were in the range £875–£1,400.

Advertisements in the *Evening News* and the *Estates Gazette* help to fill out the 1930 picture. At Ickenham Road, Uxbridge, the Unit Construction Co. were building three-bedroom semis. This popular type was also advertised as available on the Kenton Farm Estate, Kenton for £725. Rotherham Estates' Deane Estate, west of Field End Road, Eastcote, about half way between the station and the old village, was selling houses at £895 upwards, whilst T. F. Nash had started to build over the Deane Estate on the east side of Field End Road at this point, opening with a price range of £895-£1,325. This last development was described as 'three minutes from the station' (something of an exaggeration) and 'half an hour' from the City and West End, 'yet in the country' (a claim that became difficult to justify almost as soon as it was made). On the Windmill Hill Estate, Ruislip Manor, R. Cross was selling new houses and bungalows at £895 upwards and nearby, on Ruislip Manor Way, D. Jackson had semis with three bedrooms *and* a boxroom at £965. Also at Ruislip, on the Hill Farm Estate, Johnson & Wilson advertised new homes from £795. At Northwood, on the Eastbury Park Estate (Davenham Avenue), Rhys J. Rhys sought slightly more wealthy customers with four-bedroom houses at £1,350 to £1,695. Close to the railway south of Preston Road station, three-bedroom Thornborough houses were available at £660 to £925.

A 1930 advertisement for the Chiltern Court Restaurant.

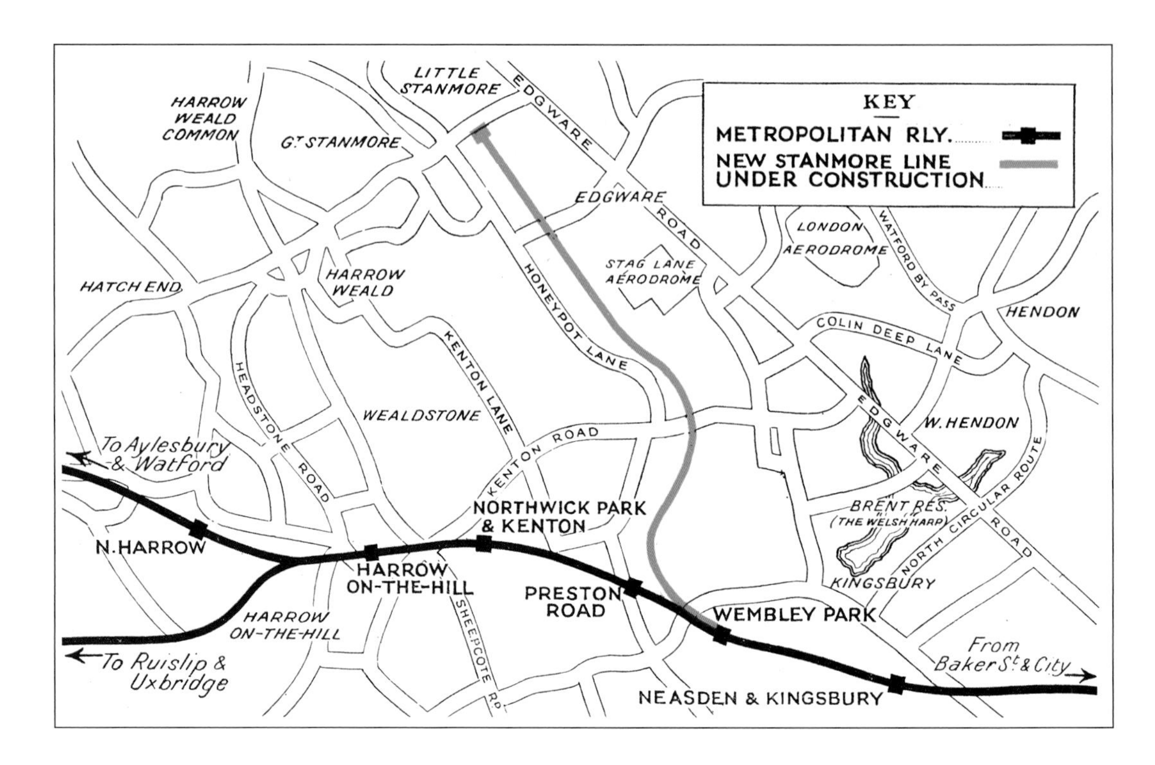

Map of the new Stanmore branch, from *Metro-land* 1931.

5 THE LAST YEARS OF METRO-LAND 1931–1933

The 1931 *Metro-land* ran to 148 pages. Amongst all the usual features was a map and an account of the new four-mile branch line being built from the Extension line between Wembley Park and Preston Road stations to terminate at Stanmore. This passed through an area of Metro-land still largely rural but not without signs of suburban development. Although the considerable housing activity eastwards around Kenton Road was now moving steadily further away from Northwick Park Metropolitan station, much of it would be within walking distance of the new line's proposed Kingsbury station.

Around Wembley Park station, the residential development was by now well advanced, including what the guide described as 'a new "Main Street" 'along the Kingsbury Road'. The text also noted that on Barn Hill, Haymills' houses 'now reach almost to the summit'. Mention was made of rapid progress on both sides of the railway at Preston Road: 'The Barn Hill Estate from the Wembley side is reaching up to the road between the station and the old hamlet of Preston' and to the south of the station 'new rows of villas stretch out towards Forty Farm and invade the fields towards Harrow. The slopes of Woodcock Hill are also filling up. The old farm house is almost lost among the crowds of newcomers.' An advertisement informed that F. & C. Costin were now building in the old hamlet of Preston on the Lyon Farm Estate, west of the Wealdstone Brook. House prices here were £1,050–£2,500.

The cover picture of the 1931 *Metro-land* depicting barges and Watford Lock on the Grand Junction Canal.

But Rayners Lane was the clearly the favourite flavour for 1931: 'Nowhere in the whole perimeter of London has more remarkable development taken place during the past year ... It repays a visit at short intervals to see it grow.' Its axis was 'the rather splendid new arterial road' being made to link Rayners Lane and North Harrow stations (Imperial Way, completed 1934). The guide noted 'Schools have begun to make their appearance, Churches and a cinema are to follow'. The cinema did not open until October 1936; originally named The Grosvenor, with 1,020 seats, it was designed by F. E. Bromige and built by T. F. Nash. It is now a listed building but no longer fulfils its original purpose.

E. S. Reid ('with a Reid house there is no such thing as monotony') now required six pages to advertise seven different types of semi-detached and two types of detached house at prices from £895 to £1,350. This firm also had shop sites available to 'afford a golden opportunity to enterprising tradesmen'. Advertising reveals three more builders at work here: Haigh Bros. in Hillcroft Avenue (semis with garage space at £955 and £975 freehold); Healey & Squire, in Hillcroft Avenue and The Avenue (three-bedroom semis at £955); and Frank Iredale in Village Way (three-bedroom semis at £975, brick garage £50 extra).

Nash 'four-blocks' on the Tithe Farm Estate south of Rayners Lane station 1932/1933. This design enabled prices to be reduced as low as £595 at early 1930s values.

AT RAYNERS LANE

Contrasts at Rayners Lane, from *Metro-land* 1931.

OAKINGTON AVENUE, HARROW GARDEN VILLAGE.

Sales were slower at the W. A. Telling Ltd Vache Estate at Chalfont St Giles, advertised as 'A BEAUTIFUL ESTATE of well Timbered Parkland adjoining Harewood Downs Golf Course. It overlooks the River Misbourn and commands charming views of the surrounding country.' Sites of one acre upwards were available and 'Residences of distinctive Designs' were stated to be in course of erection. This site was north east of the village and a long 1½ miles south of Chalfont & Latimer station, so a motor car was a desirable accessory.

In nearby Chorleywood, the Troutstream Estates were building either side of the River Chess, north of the Cedars Estate from 1930. Although they refused access to Wardle's staff, they estimated at the end of 1932 that 100 houses of a proposed 250 had been built. At the same date Wardle was able to inform Selbie that since its commencement, 466 houses and 21 shops had been completed on the MRCE Cedars Estate. It is of interest to recall that Selbie had moved to the relative safety of Chorleywood during World War 1, taking *The Orchard*, Shire Lane, a house designed by the Arts & Crafts architect C. F. A. Voysey in 1899–1900. But by the end of 1920, his name no longer appeared in the Electoral Register at this address. Perhaps his brief stay in the area had some connection with the choice of the local Cedars Estate as the major item in the MRCE's initial purchases in 1919.

Awaiting the new Railway but eager to advertise in the 1931 Metro-land was Henry J. Clare, whose Ideal Homes Estate (see below) was located at Old Church Lane, Stanmore (described by Clare as 'The New Addition to *Metro-land*'). His houses were detached and semi-detached, the price range £1,075–£3,500. At 280ft above sea level, the estate had its own tennis courts, including one hard court with 'flood lighting for all-the-year-round play'.

THE IDEAL HOMES ESTATE

THE NEW ADDITION TO METRO-LAND

STANMORE

MIDDLESEX

A RURAL DISTRICT TEN MILES FROM MARBLE ARCH

The Estate that is different

Distinctive Detached and Semi-detached Houses, all with space for Garage, from £1,075 to £3,500, Freehold. Situated in the heart of the country, yet within easy reach of the Metropolis, this Estate is, as its name implies, " Ideal " for home life. It is surrounded by open country, including the wide expanse of Stanmore Common, and many acres of sports grounds; an excellent Golf Course is adjacent, and tennis courts are available on the Estate itself, one hard court having flood lighting for all-the-year-round play. The altitude is 280 feet; gas, electric light and water services are laid on, together with main drainage; whilst the subsoil is gravelly. The City and West End are easily accessible.

No Rows of Stereotyped dwellings

All houses are soundly constructed, and, irrespective of price, have double slate damp-course; all brickwork in cement mortar; strong concrete foundations; boarded roofs under tiles; Oregon pine block flooring to ground floors; square pattern bath, completely tiled in; tiled bathroom with recessed wall fittings; pedestal lavatory basin; slow combustion stove giving constant hot water; gas or electric power points to choice, and electric light throughout, completely decorated ready for occupation; inclusive of all paths and close boarded fences.

A postcard will ensure immediate delivery of an illustrated booklet of plans and photographs of all types of houses, and a saloon car is always at the disposal of intending purchasers.

HENRY J. CLARE BUILDER AND CONTRACTOR TELEPHONES STANMORE 344 & 345

Off Headstone Lane, opposite the 60-acre Headstone Manor Recreation Ground, Thomas Higgs' Holmdene Estate on 'Clean concrete roads already made' did its bit to fill the remaining open land between North Harrow and Pinner stations. Here three-bedroom semis sold at £995 and four-bedroom types at £1,150–£1,400. Some filling-in was still possible north of the railway at North Harrow, hence an advertisement for the Kingsfield Avenue Estate by A. J. King, with houses priced at £875–£1,400, over 60 of which had already been purchased by Harrow residents.

On the other side of Harrow, east of the Euston line but within walking distance of Northwick Park station, Geo. H. Gillett & Co. were building semis and detached houses priced at £975–£1,525 in Woodcock Hill Lane.

At Ruislip, H. L. Bowers advertised the Croft Estate, three minutes from the station, semis with three bedrooms at £985 freehold and four bedrooms at £1,175, all with garage space. Bowers also went into the new cheaper end of the market at Ruislip Station Estate on the other side of the tracks (see page 108).

Within the catchment area of the new station at Watford, building was still in progress on the Cassiobury Park (see right) and Dell Field Estates, four advertisements offering semis and detached types, mostly with four bedrooms from £1,010 upwards.

Outer Metro-land still attracted the ramblers and what Wardle's office called 'Pleasure Parties and Pleasure Seekers'; for the latter, a free booklet *A Day in The Country* (page 102) was available, showing detailed particulars of the countryside, with information regarding cheap fare facilities.

Cassiobury Park Estate
WATFORD

Within Five Minutes' Walk of Metropolitan and L.N.E. Extension Terminus and Ten Minutes' of the L.M.S. Watford Junction. TRAVEL FACILITIES to all parts and to London. GOLF COURSES.—The following are within easy distance of the Estate: West Herts, Moor Park, Oxhey, Sandy Lodge, Bushey Hall, Northwood, and Grimm's Dyke, Hatch End.

A BUILDING ESTATE OFFERING MANY ADVANTAGES AND INDUCEMENTS TO PURCHASERS

Though close to the important Shopping Centre of Watford the Estate stands in the midst of charming, unspoilt country. It comprises the site where stood Cassiobury Mansion with its beautiful and extensive grounds and woodlands and overlooks the pleasant valley of the Gade. Its position is extremely healthy, on gravel soil, about 230 feet above sea. Main Drainage is provided to the new roads, and Water, Gas and Electric Light Services are available. The site offers great facilities for speedy building, and Cassiobury Estates, Ltd., are prepared to grant easy terms for payment when required, while the Watford Corporation possess an excellent scheme for granting financial assistance to those building or buying houses in the Borough. For particulars of houses already built on the Cassiobury Estate apply direct to all or any of the builders on the next few pages.

Full particulars of Land for Sale on application to:

The Secretary, Cassiobury Estates, Ltd., Carlton Chambers, Clarendon Rd., Watford

'Phone: Watford 1212 & 1213.

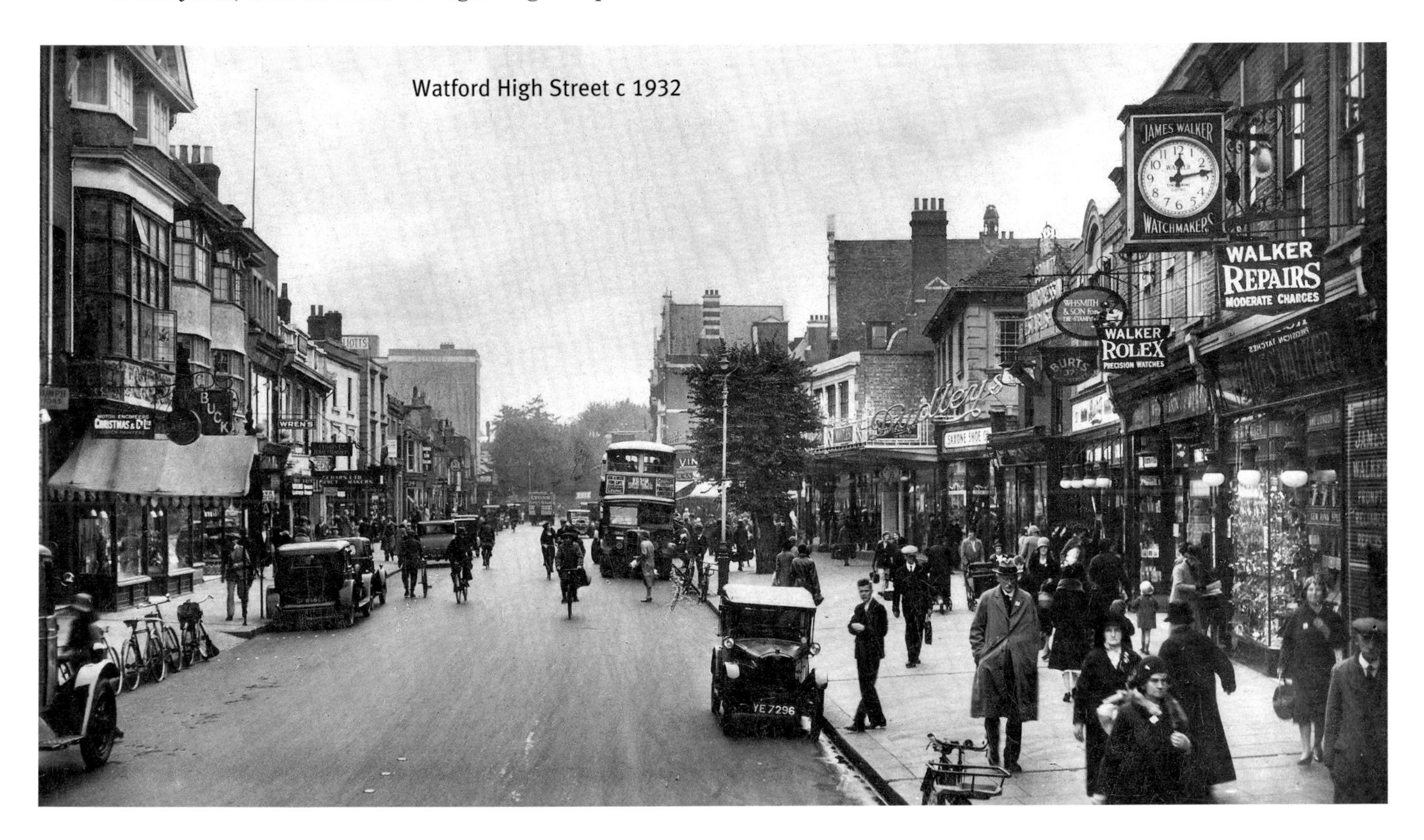

Watford High Street c 1932

A DAY IN THE
COUNTRY

Spare space in the advertisement section of the 1931 *Metro-land* was used to recommend the *Country Walks* booklets, still only twopence and 'obtainable at any Metro. station'. By this means ramblers could 'readily find their way, without reference to map, or need for enquiry, into the most charming and intimate rural recesses . . .' Below this announcement, amateur photographers were cordially invited to submit their photos of rural scenes in Metro-land for reproduction in the Company's publicity; a fee of 7s 6d was offered for each picture accepted. Some of the respondents were the proprietors of places of refreshment advertised on *Metro-land* and examples of this work are held by London's Transport Museum.

Residential developments advertised in the *Evening News*, the *Estates Gazette* and elsewhere help to fill out the 1931 situation. As mentioned earlier, there was already some activity in the districts soon to be served by the new Stanmore branch: at Canons Park Estate, (F. W. Bristow, £1,300 upwards); at Kingsbury, Roe Green, Kingsbury Road; at Kenton Road, corner of Shrewsbury Avenue (A. J. Cowper £745–£895); and at Fairfields Heights Estate, Roe Green (Smith Bros. £925 upwards). At Queensbury, Stag Lane, Fairway Avenue, houses were available at £750.

West of this, at Kenton, on the Glebe Farm Estate, (Morland Gardens, etc.) Smith Bros. had new houses from £775 upwards and along D'Arcy Gardens were W. H. Elliott's three-bedroom semis at £740. At Harrow, Dudley Gardens, Johnston & Black were offering houses at £875. Cutler was still busy filling up his very own North Harrow, some of which could be described as 'Pinner'. His prices now ran from £795-£895 for semis, for detached houses from £950, these in Mount Drive, Station Road and Pinner Village Estate. Also at North Harrow, Suffolk Road, H. Pickerill was selling semis and detached houses at £850 upwards.

In the new suburb of Northwood Hills, Belton Estates Ltd in Potter Street were advertising semis at £700–£850 and detached houses at £920. Further out (27 minutes from Baker Street) in Parkway and Fieldway, Rickmansworth, were J. W. Minett's houses, semis from £790 to £1,050 and detached at £950 to £1,375, the higher prices securing four bedrooms and two lavatories. All had garages or garage space.

At Hillingdon on the Palace Estate (Denecroft Crescent etc.), Stedman & Clarke were offering small houses at £595, each provided with a stone from Buckingham Palace to carry the house name. These probably came from a job lot which had been lying in a builders' yard since the east front of the Palace was replaced in 1913.

A 1931 view of T F Nash shops in Kenton Road at the southern edge of their estate, close to Kenton (LMSR) and Northwick Park (Metropolitan) stations.

Rayners Lane in March 1934, looking to Uxbridge, still very much the old wooden Metropolitan halt with just one sign of its new ownership. Heedless of risk, men in caps squat precariously to work at the platform edge amid the waiting passengers, one using a wood saw. A poster announces Gracie Fields's latest film *Love, Life and Laughter* at London's Coliseum Theatre.

1932–33: Metro-land's last days

For what was to be the last edition of *Metro-land*, Michael Reilly provided another pleasing cover (p.105), an impression of a path through a wood of tall birch trees in which he again mixed sunlight and shadow with consummate skill.

The book's 148 pages contained all the usual features, with substantial passages of text repeated once more from earlier editions. A piece about the new line to Stanmore headed *The Metro's Latest Project* was mostly written in the future tense since the branch did not open for public services until 10 December 1932. For the ceremonial opening on the previous day, Wardle arranged for British Movietone News to make a sound film and his staff also prepared a souvenir booklet, *Stanmore's New Railway*, for the press representatives and guests.

Earlier, on 10 January 1932, the Metropolitan had completed the quadrupling of its tracks between Wembley Park and Harrow South Junction, a project which required rebuilding Northwick Park and Preston Road stations and allowed improvements in the train service to handle the substantial growth in traffic generated by the spread of new housing across the inner and central zones of Metro-land.

Metro-land recorded that on the south side of the line at Preston Road, suburban development was now 'practically linked up with Wembley Park'; the Harrow Golf Club, adjoining the Railway, had been taken over as building land.

Michael
Reilly.
METRO-LAND
PRICE TWO-PENCE

The last fields on the slopes of Woodcock Hill (Kenton) were being laid out for building and the SLC's Woodcock Dell Estate, next to Selfridge's Sports Ground, already had a 'score of pleasant villas' on its 8½-acre site where plots at £150 upwards were available for further building. Lyon's farmhouse in Preston Road survived the rolling tide of small houses and was not demolished until 1960 but most of its land had passed to the speculative builder long before. The farm bore the name of John Lyon, founder of Harrow School, but the house was rebuilt after his death in 1592.

According to the guide, the catchment area of Northwick Park & Kenton station had in the previous five years grown at almost 1,000 houses a year but we must remember that some of the resulting traffic would have gone to the LMSR and Underground services at Kenton station. The whole area north of the line between Wembley Park and Harrow was now already well on the way to becoming a close-packed expanse of new housing, mostly semis, and the guide is obliged to resort to a reference to the golf course south of the railway as 'happily' securing the amenities of this district, a pathetic stretch of rural Metro-land somehow surviving. Fishing around desperately for something positive to say in conclusion, the writer unblushingly suggested the area between the Metropolitan Railway and Kenton 'might well serve other local authorities as a model of town planning'.

North Harrow station had been rebuilt in 1930–31, since the halt had become quite inadequate for the traffic Cutler and other house builders were now presenting twice daily for travel to and from central London. The area had grown into a new suburb, mainly of semis, with its own 1,500-seat cinema (1928) and shopping parade on the Harrow–Pinner Road. This last, according to the *Metro-land* scribe was now 'a broad and comely High Street' and either side of the railway here 'attractive

Wembley Park station 1933, looking north to Haymills' Barn Hill Estate (follow the arrow, left).

avenues are being laid out with pleasant vistas' (of other attractive avenues?) The Embassy cinema, built alongside the Yeading Brook, too close to a hastily filled-in pond, was to suffer serious subsidence in 1936, opening up major cracks in the auditorium and causing closure for reconstruction. Shops here included branches of W. H. Cullen (grocers), Express Dairies (including a waitress-service restaurant), Home & Colonial (grocers) and United Dairies. The last had taken over from the first occupier, who had sold milk from the fast disappearing local farms across a marble counter surrounded by tiled walls.

Rayner's Lane and North Harrow were already closing up together and *Metro-land* tried hard to cheer up any who had regrets about the loss of 'the quiet rustic beauty' of the old Rayner's Lane by mentioning that 'the broad streets of the new suburb are being beautified by the planting of trees'. E. S. Reid was now advertising a choice of no fewer than 16 different types of house in the area bounded by Rayner's Lane, Farm Avenue, The Drive and Oakington Avenue. Reid claimed that rather than uprooting existing trees and hedges, he would re-position his houses, which may explain some variations in the building line. Newcomers to the 'Garden Village' were B. D. Bird & Sons, offering semis of fairly standard style in The Greenway at £850.

Eastcote was now well on the path to suburban transformation. Four hundred new houses had been built by this time and *Metro-land* stated 'preparations have been made for another two thousand.' At the Cannon Croft Estate, almost equidistant from Pinner and Eastcote stations, the General Housing Co. Ltd advertised semis at £825 freehold and on the Eastcote Hill Estate, houses were now ready at prices from £975 freehold. The poplar-lined country lane between the station and Eastcote village was giving way to a line of shops.

No. 2
THIS BOOKLET IS ONE OF A SERIES OF FOUR
TWENTY-FOURTH EDITION
COUNTRY WALKS
IN
MIDDLESEX
HERTFORDSHIRE AND
BUCKINGHAMSHIRE
WITH
SKETCH MAPS OF ROUTES
ISSUED BY THE METROPOLITAN AND LONDON & NORTH EASTERN RAILWAYS
PRICE 2D

Pinner station Up side, 1933. This is the original building of 1885, at this time retaining many of its original features internally. The exterior is in yellow brick with blue brick ornament and pink mortar, under a slate roof.

Much the same process was under way at nearby Ruislip, where *Metro-land* noted 'the little township is growing rapidly in all directions'. One direction was south of the railway, on the Station Estate (Eversley Crescent, etc.), where H. L. Bowers (who also provided more expensive accommodation on the other side of the tracks for 'gentle folk') now advertised six-block units as low as £695 freehold (see left), offering free travel vouchers from any London station to those wishing to inspect them. This type of construction, combining four, six or even eight units in one block cut building costs; combined with more intensive use of land and smaller room sizes, it enabled prices to be reduced quite drastically. Bowers was one of the first to introduce it to Metro-land. One of Bower's brochures speaks of an ancient sage, who after wandering far in search of happiness found it, at last, at his own door. "So it is with houses, for right close at hand – at Ruislip, 24 minutes journey from Town – the dream house you have yearned for is waiting ready to be secured at a price easily within your reach."

At Hillingdon, the guide records a similar transformation to that now visible at Ruislip and Eastcote, with nearly 2,000 houses built and sold in the previous few years. In this edition, the Hillingdon Estates Co. Ltd advertised 'really wonderful well-built seven-room residences' at £725 freehold, claimed as 'built to sell at a much higher price' as if they were items in a department store's summer sale. This company also offered houses to rent from £49 to £55 a year, possibly a sign that at this time sales were sluggish. Also at Hillingdon, on the Highfields Estate, 'A Model Tudor Village', five minutes' walk from the station, the Tudor Housing Co. (left) were advertising semis and detached types 'artistically grouped in the form of fascinating courts'. These were sold from £995 freehold.

Returning to the Extension line, Pinner was reported as 'still spreading fast', its Headstone Farm now 'almost swallowed up by the houses which have arisen around it'. Further out, there was more building activity. though none of it on a scale comparable to what was happening nearer to London; a 'new residential quarter' was noted as appearing around Chalfont & Latimer station, in an area 'which will soon require a name of its own'. In addition building was taking place nearby on the Nightingale, Pollards Park, Beechwood and Old House Farm Estates. The 'new Amersham on the level ground near the station' was reported as 'spreading fast in all directions'. Further still down the line, Great Missenden was said to be developing fast on the Prestwood and Kingswood side.

Reference to advertising in London newspapers and other sources gives a more complete picture of housebuilding in Metro-land in this final period of the life of the Metropolitan Railway. We need to look first at two areas where new railway facilities and suburban development were closely interwoven and interdependent.

Pinner c 1930. Top; High Street looking NE. This street is described in the 1932 *Metro-land* as 'The most picturesque feature of the little town'. Bridge Street (centre: looking north west, bottom: looking south east) displays a mix of plain Victorian and early 20th century mock Tudor and neo-Georgian styles.

A new suburb was emerging between Pinner and Northwood, an area where there had been agitation for a station since 1922. At the beginning of 1931 around 390 acres near the railway had become available for housebuilding and with construction of some 3,000 houses in prospect, the pressure for railway services was renewed. By the autumn of that year, 215 houses had been erected north of the line and in January 1932 Hooper advertised The Hundred Acre Estate, Northwood Way, with four-bedroomed semis at £945-£1125. George Ball had three-bedroom semis in the same location from £875. Along Potter Street and at Lyndhurst Avenue at the end of 1932, Edward Quirk was offering semis at £695 and £725 and small detached types at £775.

Meanwhile negotiations with estate developers and builders had secured agreement that they would not only guarantee the Metropolitan a minimum annual revenue of £947 but would also find half the £12,000 cost of the station they needed to ensure maximum return from their outlay on residential development.

The resulting traffic was such that the guarantors were at no risk and since it was estimated a station would raise the value of the land by around £80 an acre, it was by no means a a bad deal for the developers. To find a name for the place and the station, the guarantors and a local newspaper organised a competition, selecting 'Northwood Hills' for the cash prize. The station, a modest structure, the last railway building designed by Charles Clark, was opened on 13 November 1933 after the Metropolitan had been taken over by the new London Passenger Transport Board. During 1933, more new housing appeared north of the railway: on the Pinner Hill Farm Estate, (P. Rains, bungalows, £625–£850, houses £795–£825); and along the Pinner Road on the Hundred Acres Farm Estate (W. Howell, semis at £875).

Joel Street looks totally rural in this 1931 view of the point where it crosses over the railway but the hoarding announces SITE FOR NEW STATION FREQUENT TRAIN SERVICES to LONDON CITY & WEST END. The photo on page 111 shows the new Northwood Hills station in November 1936 looking north towards shopping parades built in 1933 each side of Joel Street.

METROPOLITAN AND
GREAT CENTRAL JOINT
COMMITTEE

NEW STATION

NORTHWOOD HILLS

OPEN 13th NOVEMBER, 1933

PARTICULARS OF TRAIN SERVICE,
SEASON TICKET RATES TO BAKER
STREET AND MARYLEBONE AND
CHEAP DAY RETURN FARES

10285 /9 /33 3,500

TRAIN SERVICE FROM NORTHWOOD HILLS

SEE MAP

To BAKER STREET				To MARYLEBONE		
WEEKDAYS				WEEKDAYS		
A.M.	P.M.	P.M.	P.M.	A.M.	P.M.	P.M.
6 18	12 4 38	4 6 SO 9 SX 24 SX	7 7 SO 13 SX 54	7 26 56	12 34	4 30 43 SO
7 1 20 50	1 12 SO 13 SX 33 SO 47 SO	5 13 25 SX 33 42 SX	8 5 SX 35	8 29 55A	1 41	6 40 SX
8 55	2 4 SO 31 56 SO	6 12 SO 16 SX 36 SO	9 12 57	9 40	2 11 SX 14 SO	7 28 43
10 1 WO 55	3 20 SX		11 33	11 27	3 36	8 11 35A 58
SUNDAYS				SUNDAYS		
A.M.	P.M.	P.M.	P.M.	A.M.	P.M.	P.M.
8 22	12 42	4 22	9 10 49	9 37	12 22	6 31
9 2 22	1 2 42	5 22 58	10 23 58		1 42 A	7 13 52
10 22	2 22	8 2 42	11 32		4 58	9 21 33 49 A
11 2 42	3 2 42					

A—Change at Harrow on the Hill B—Change at Pinner

As mentioned earlier, developers and speculative builders were busy in its catchment area some time before the new Stanmore branch, with its intermediate stations at Kingsbury and Canons Park (Edgware), was opened for business on 10 December 1932. Indeed, at Kingsbury, the Metropolitan was involved in unforeseen expenditure when constructing the formation of the new railway since the engineers found they had to cut through planned estate roads and new sewers north of the main road. Within a year of the line's opening the area around Kingsbury station had become a suburban centre with shopping parades and a 1,000-seat cinema.

A fourth station, Queensbury, stipulated as a condition of sale by the landowners, All Souls College, Oxford, had to await development of its main catchment area, which although planned, could not seriously begin until the closure and sale of Stag Lane Airfield in late 1933. This station was not opened until 16 December 1934, well into the London Transport era.

Semis with garage space at £950 on the The Valley Farm Estate, just south east of Kingsbury station, were first advertised by A. M. Haddow in April and May 1932 and another development close to the station site was announced by D. Todd in June (three-bedroom semis from £795). The Audley Estate, also near the new station, was developed by A. F. Davis (later Davis Estates) with three-bedroom semis at only £665 advertised from May 1932. This firm later extended its activities to other parts of London.

At Canons Park, the first estates, built by Laing and D. C. Houses from 1933, were west of the new line. The Ideal Homes Estate (page 100) was even further west, close to the older Harrow–Stanmore branch, built and first operated by the LNWR.

One important and extensive housing development started at the very end of the Metropolitan Railway era remains to be mentioned. At Rayners Lane, south of the railway, T. F. Nash began to advertise their 250-acre Tithe Farm Estate in November 1932, quoting £595 for a 2½-bedroom unit in a terrace block and a price range of £650–£785 for semis. Some 3,500 houses were to be erected here, many at the high density of 12 to the acre in terrace blocks of four or six. Construction materials were brought from Rayners Lane freight yard by horse-drawn carts, motor trucks and over an extensive system of temporary narrow gauge light railways operated with small petrol locomotives. This estate extended for almost a mile south of Rayners Lane, its southern extremities closer to South Harrow Metropolitan District Railway station, where the Metropolitan made an end-on junction at the country end of the platforms.

A new Metro-land suburb. Kingsbury Road, looking east to Kingsbury station (extreme right), c 1935. The Odeon Cinema, designed by A Percival Starkey, was opened on 30 May 1934 and had over 1,000 seats.

With several mentions of the 'Metro.' but none of *Metro-Land*, this advertisement appeared in the 1933 *Railway Yearbook*.

AT LONDON'S ELBOW

A BRIEF and inexpensive journey on the Metropolitan Railway will lead the pleasure-seeker into some of the most delightful scenery to be found in England, and those who visit it for the first time will be enchanted with its many attractions, whilst those who know it well will never tire of its charms.

The districts served boast of many places of historic interest, famous view-points and spacious parks; it abounds in old-world villages and haunts of ancient peace, and there are also a multitude of out-of-the-way nooks and corners to be found where the life of the countryside is proof against the changes that have overwhelmed it elsewhere.

The train service provided by the Metro. is unrivalled for frequency and speed, and the cheap fares issued for the benefit of pleasure-seekers are both low in cost and liberal in range. Special arrangements are also made for parties, for whom, in the case of large numbers, reserved accommodation, without any additional charge, is provided.

The roads throughout are good and well adapted for cycling, and for those who find joy in country rambles there are field-paths and wood-paths in rich and varied abundance. In this connection the Metro. issue a series of "Country Walks" booklets, containing a wide range of lucidly described rambles, amplified by carefully drawn sketch maps, and these may be readily obtained, price 2d., at any Metro. Booking Office or Bookstall.

For further particulars of cheap fares, pleasure party arrangements, catering facilities, train services, etc., apply to the Commercial Manager, Baker Street Station, N.W.1, who will gladly supply the fullest information.

BAKER ST. STATION, N.W.1. J. S. ANDERSON, General Manager.

As Metro-land faded from the scene, almost all the grass plain west of the Nash Tithe Farm Estate and south of the Harrow–Uxbridge line remained untouched by the builders but within the ensuing seven years, most of it would be covered with small houses built by George Ball's Manor Homes, G.T. Crouch, Davis Estates, Taylor Woodrow and others.

This process was not untypical. The disappearance of the Metropolitan Railway and its Metro-land offspring in 1933 broadly coincided with a significant change in the way in which much new residential development around London was provided. As we have seen, a great deal of the new building across Metro-land had been undertaken by numerous small firms, most of them restricting their activity to a narrowly defined area. Some of these small developers became victims of the economic depression of the early 1930s.

Others, such as Cutler, Comben & Wakeling and F. & C. Costin were strong enough to survive but wisely kept to locations they knew best. Nash and Davis, both starting in Metro-land, were to extend their activities to other parts of the London outskirts, as did Haymills. At the same time, the area we have been considering was about to be invaded by larger enterprises such as Laing, Wimpey, Taylor Woodrow and Crouch, businesses able to take advantage of economies of scale and bring down prices.

An artist's impression of furnished kitchen, sitting room and dining room of a house on the T F Nash Tithe Farm Estate, Rayners Lane (from the firm's 1933 brochure).

The modest ticket office and entrance provided for Hillingdon station when it was opened on 10 December 1923. Until the station was rebuilt in 1931, the facilities here soon proved inadequate for the passenger traffic arising from the large amount of new housing erected nearby from 1922, most of it south of the line as far as the Uxbridge Road.

At Ruislip Manor (opened 5 August 1912), the provision was initially similar to that at Hillingdon but here the first residential development was stifled by the upheaval of the 1914–18 War and housebuilding did not really accelerate until 1932–33, notably south of the line. Traffic then justified a new station building, opened in 1938. In this 1933 view, construction of a shopping parade is seen in progress south of the railway bridge.

Kingsbury; a new station on a new branch, seen in 1933.

Metro-land matured: Uxendon Crescent (near Preston Road station) on the Haymills Barn Hill Estate. The Hill (282ft above sea level) appears in the background.

A Metro-land suburb completed. Imperial Drive, North Harrow, soon after the 1934 opening of this new road to Rayners Lane. The view looks north east to the railway bridge, with North Harrow station at its left end, and in the background the roof of the Embassy Cinema in Pinner Road rises above a shopping parade. At the left, commuters in dark suits can be seen coming up from the station on their way home to their mortgaged Cutler semis.

1933–1947: A 'Devastating Onrush' checked

Although the Metropolitan Railway was no more, the unrelenting expansion of suburban London continued apace until it was brought to a sudden halt by the outbreak of World War 2 towards the end of 1939. Had the company survived for those few years, there is no doubt that the management would have welcomed and encouraged a steadily advancing tide of new housing beyond Rickmansworth and north of Ruislip; indeed the tide might well have been much more vigorous than it actually was. We can be confident that if the old guard had still been in the Baker Street offices in 1938–39 they would have actively supported the appearance at that time of the beginnings of a new estate between Shire Lane and the railway at the country end of Chorleywood station. This came complete with Main Way (now Whitelands Avenue) extending alongside the tracks, ready to push further and link Chorleywood West with the neighbouring community around Chalfont & Latimer station, a coalescence only stopped by Britain's entry into the war.

Such uncontrolled expansion was possible because until the passage of the post-war Labour Government's Town & Country Planning Act in 1947, there was no statutory continuous Green Belt around Greater London and territorial planning was non-existent outside the inner zone controlled by the London County Council.

The Metropolitan Railway Country Estates Ltd continued to trade from Baker Street station, having become a separate company from 29th June 1933, three days before the Metropolitan Railway was swallowed up by the London Passenger Transport Board. This advertisement is from the August 1937 edition of *Homes and Gardens*.

Such planning provisions as did exist placed the primary responsibility on local councils, bodies too inward-looking, too weak financially to afford compensation payments to secure planning decisions and far too numerous for effective co-operation. It was a situation vividly and lucidly described by Dr W. A. Robson, Reader in Administrative Law and later Professor of Public Administration, University of London. When giving evidence to the Royal Commission on the Geographical Distribution of the Industrial Population on 15 June 1938 he spoke of how London's pleasant countryside had been covered with thousands of new houses of all descriptions, 'the devastating onrush of the speculative builder, aided and abetted in one notorious instance by a railway company turned landowner', a process which no local authority 'even pretended to regulate and guide for the common good'. The 1947 Act mentioned in the previous paragraph enabled county councils and county boroughs to block any development proposal in specified areas with compensation paid by central government, thus permitting the establishment of a continuous all-purpose Green Belt around the capital for the first time. This had been a major component of Professor Patrick Abercrombie's Greater London Plan, 1944, a document which included some interesting information and recommendations regarding certain parts of Metro-land (see Appendix 3).

HOMES IN N

SEEING IS BELIEVING

Seeing is believing and you have only to come and see for yourself how different the Reid house is, to be convinced right away of their wonderful value. Every house reflects consummate care and thoroughness of workmanship; every house possesses an individuality of its own, whilst, thanks to a convenient system of repayment, you can buy one for less than it would cost to rent. Prices from £895 to £1,600—come and see them this week-end. Cheap tickets to Rayners Lane from all stations.

E. S. REID, Station Estate Office, Harrow Garden Village, Middlesex.

(Telephone: Pinner 987.) Adjoining Rayners Lane Station.

Type "D" House, £

NORTH HARROW & PINNER VILLAG

(Adjoining NEW PUBLIC PARK)

SOUNDLY BUILT HOUSES AND BUNGALOWS. ALL WITH GARAGE SPACE.

Semi-detached houses from **£695** Freehold Larger types **£750** and **£**
Detached from **£950**. Bungalows ready shortly, **£650.** 90 per cent. mort
arranged with low repayments. Reduced payment terms now availa
NO ROAD CHARGES or LAW COSTS Artistically designed, thorou
labour-saving. Low season ticket rates. Inspect houses at any time or
your own Surveyor. Over 1,700 houses built and sold in this dist
Write to-day for full particulars.

CUTLERS LTD., 14 STATION ROAD, NORTH HARR

Builders at North Harrow for over 20 years. ('Phone: Harrow 0139.)

WATFORD'S BIGGEST BARGAIN

At the amazingly low figure of **15/11** a week you can buy, on the delightful Kingswood Estate, Sheepcote Lane, Watford, a superior seven-room H.E.C. house of which you could be proud for all time. The accommodation comprises an attractive Entrance Hall; 2 spacious Reception Rooms; a perfect labour-saving Kitchen; 3 well-proportioned Bedrooms; a tastefully tiled Bathroom with "Shower" device, a separate W.C. and a host of outstanding features. There are no road charges, legal costs or "Extras" of any kind, and the all-in Freehold price is only **£590,** whilst a nominal deposit will secure possession. Come and see them this week-end, or send for descriptive folder. Frequent bus service from all parts of Watford.

KINGSWOOD ESTATE, SHEEPCOTE LANE, ST. ALBAN'S ROAD, WATFORD.

SOLE AGENTS: HILL, KING & CO., WESTMINSTER BANK CHAMBERS, WATFORD.

"COSTIN" HOUSES AT KENTO

WOODCOCK DELL £775 LYON FARM £1,00

and upwards—FREEHOLD.

Built of finest materials. Individual designs. Labour Saving devices. L
Gardens. Electric Light Fittings included. Exceptional Train Service—
Station on Estate. No Road, Paving or Legal Charges. Write for Boo

DEPOSITS from £45. REPAYMENTS from 22/6 WEEK

F. & C. COSTIN, LTD., KENTON, MIDDLESEX.

Telephone: Wordsworth 2244 and 2245. Also Private Extensions.

THE CEDARS ESTATE, RICKMANSWORTH

Offers something better than is usually found, and is just that higher class district which attracts. The subsoil is gravel and sand, and the countryside is well wooded and undulating, thus giving its best in charm and beauty. Within 26 minutes journey to London; low Season Ticket rates. Detached Residences, different in design and size, and each standing in ample grounds, are offered from **£995** to **£2,350** Freehold. A NEW DEVELOPMENT OF SEMI-DETACHED AND DETACHED HOUSES, each with spacious rooms and garage, from **£825** to **£1,125**. Deposit only **£25** to include stamp duties. OVERLOOKING MOOR PARK—Bungalow residences from **£1,250** Freehold—Deposit only **£50.**
Illustrated handbook free on application to

H. GIBSON, The Metropolitan Railway Country Estates, Limited,
Baker Street Station, N.W.1. (Telephone: Welbeck 6688.)

HARROW GARDEN VILLAG

£680
Freehold.
Total Deposit: £25
No Stamp Duties. No Mortgage Costs.

These semi-detached properties, all of which are situa
within 5 minutes walk of Rayners Lane Station, o
extraordinary value, and the demand for them is exceptio
The ground floor comprises, Front Room, 17 ft. 6 ins. x 11 ft. 6i
Back Room 15 ft. x 13 ft., large Kitchen, built-in Gara
First floor: 2 Bedrooms 14 ft. 6 ins. x 11 ft. and 11 ft. 6 ins. x 11
Box room 10 ft. 6 ins. x 8 ft., Tiled Bathroom, separate W.C.
Others with enlarged first floor at £695 freehold. Detached Bungalows also avail
from £690 freehold. For further particulars apply—

H. GIBSON, The Metropolitan Railway Country Estates, Limit
Baker Street Station, N.W.1. (Telephone: Welbeck 6

This advert records a curious interlude in 1933 when, briefly, housing in Metro-land was advertised by the Publicity Manager of the new London Passenger Transport Board still employing the term 'Metro-land' and in one case, distributing leaflets inherited from the Metropolitan Railway. This may have been arranged simply to cover the brief interval whilst the former Metropolitan property subsidiaries secured their new independent status.

ETRO-LAND

ROBINSON'S LATEST TYPE

The keenest bargain in house-property since the War £750 buys above superior, full-size, seven-room, freehold Robinson house with tiled bathroom and kitchen; panelled bath, etc., etc. Wonderfully well built; excellently appointed. Large rooms, spacious garden, attractive frontage and room for garage. Lose no time in inspecting the supply is limited, the demand keen. Also wide range of other desirable types of houses available at keen prices. Send to-day for descriptive booklet. Estate immediately adjoins Rayners Lane Station. Unique train service. Low Season Ticket Rates, cheap tickets from all stations.

A. ROBINSON, BUILDER, HARROW GARDEN VILLAGE, MIDDLESEX.
(Telephone: Pinner 995). Adjoining Rayners Lane Station.

KENTON

(15 minutes from BAKER STREET)

FREEHOLD £695

Modern in every respect, soundly built, and beautifully finished, with a constructional guarantee in the Contract.

Repayments to Building Society

Per **17/10** Week

EDWARDS

Adjoining L.M.S. and Bakerloo Station.
Tel.: Wordsworth 2257.

TOTAL DEPOSIT £35

No other charges whatsoever

Low Rates and Taxes **4/1** per week

Cheap Electricity **4d.** per unit

Gas - **9d.** per therm

CHOOSE A HADDOW HOUSE

VALLEY FARM ESTATE, KINGSBURY, N.W.9.

£925 Freehold. ...ce for Garage. Deposit from £60 Legal or Survey Fees.

Here is a 3 Bedroomed Semi-detached house of ultra modern design that cannot fail to attract. Situated on a well planned Estate adjoining Kingsbury Station. These Houses prove a sound investment and appreciate in value. Compare the Kitchen with any house you have seen, as only one of the excellent features, and you will get an idea of competitive values. Electric Fires fitted in Bedrooms. Parquet Floor in Hall. All in Standard price. Call at once, Phone or write to the Actual Builders

A. & M. HADDOW, Valley Farm Estate, Kingsbury, N.W.9
(Phone: Colindale 6920).

Type 18 Price £1,550 Freehold.

EASTBURY PARK, NORTHWOOD

(Off Davenham Avenue and Eastbury Avenue). A GOLFER'S PARADISE.

NORTHWOOD—The finest residential area in Metro-land, altitude 400 ft., and a Golfer's paradise. The Eastbury Park Estate adjoins Sandy Lodge, Moor Park and Northwood Golf Courses, and is within ten minutes' walk of Northwood Station and the New Merchant Taylors' School. Houses of different design, embodying the latest ideas, with 3, 4 or more Bedrooms, 2 W.C.'s, tiled Kitchen, all fitments built in; cavity walls, boarded roof, every modern innovation, and built to superior specification under personal supervision. Prices from £1,250 Freehold, with Garage. New Concrete Roads. Rates approx. 8/- in the £. Deposits from 10 %. Write, 'phone or call for full particulars and illustrated brochure.

RHYS J. REES & CO., LTD., Estate Office, Davenham Avenue, NORTHWOOD
('PHONE: NORTHWOOD 963 - Office Open Week-ends).

WELLER ESTATE, AMERSHAM

NO ROAD CHARGES. NO STAMP DUTIES. NO SURVEYOR'S FEES.

£875 Freehold. Total Deposit: £25

These artistically designed 3 Bedroom Semi-detached Houses are beautifully situated in New Amersham, near the Common and Chesham Bois, 3 minutes from the Railway Station and a minute of the shops. Also with 4 large Bedrooms at **£985 freehold** and detached **£1,200.** Semi-Bungalows **£695.** All have a built-in Garage. A rare opportunity to secure a property in the glorious Chilterns, yet only 40 minutes from Town. Write for Illustrated particulars from:

. GIBSON, The Metropolitan Railway Country Estates, Limited,
...aker Street Station, N.W. 1. (Telephone: Welbeck 6688.)

CANNON CROFT ESTATE, PINNER

Only a few minutes' walk from Pinner station. Chalet Bungalows £795 Freehold. 3 bedrooms, 2 reception rooms, w.c., tiled bathroom and tiled kitchen. Cupboard accommodation for everything. Large storage cupboard, 3 wardrobe cupboards, heated linen cupboard, hat and coat cupboard in hall, large larder. Other types of semi-detached houses from £750. Detached from £950. Equipment includes electric light fittings and shades, fitted kitchen cabinet, enamelled domestic boiler and gas copper, enclosed bath, pedestal basin, electric wall points, gas points, etc. Good gardens with room for garage. Close boarded fences. NO LAW COSTS. NO ROAD CHARGES.

Estate Office: Eastcote Road, Pinner. (Pinner 1053).

BUILDERS: THE GENERAL HOUSING COMPANY LIMITED
58 Birch Grove, ACTON, W.3. (Acorn 3897.)

6 RETROSPECT

Selbie did not survive to oversee the last years of the Metropolitan Railway; he collapsed and died in St Paul's Cathedral on 17 May 1930 whilst attending a Confirmation service at which his younger son was a candidate. The story of the Company's final years, the struggle of the board and management he left behind to maintain the Metropolitan's independence in the face of government proposals to set up a new body to control London's passenger transport has been told elsewhere.[1] Suffice to say here that at midnight on 30 June 1933 the Metropolitan Railway Company ceased to exist, replaced by the London Passenger Transport Board, an organisation dominated by the former Underground Group led by Lord Ashfield and Frank Pick. They had no remit to maintain the network of property subsidiaries and the Metro-land concept, that word being firmly and totally banished from all official usage after a brief overlap. Both the SLC and the MRCE, excluded from the bodies to be transferred to the LPTB, were left to continue independently. On 29 June 1933 the SLC was incorporated as a separate public property investment company, the Metropolitan Railway Surplus Lands Company Ltd, to acquire the SLC undertaking. The MRCE became a separate company engaged in UK-wide development and for many years both bodies shared the same offices.

As an effective generator of lucrative new traffic, Selbie's property policies, built on his inheritance from Watkin and others, must be considered an outstanding success, assisted as they undoubtedly were by his encouragement of Wardle's very enthusiastic, if unsophisticated publicity machine, *Metro-land* et al.

Brave attempts to organise developments that would be attractive to those able to afford First Class seasons and ordinary tickets, such as that on the Rickmansworth Cedars Estate, may have proved disappointing, with plots and houses selling only slowly in the years before 1933, but this was no different from the experience of most independent concerns entering the same market at this time. Elsewhere on the Railway's own estates, the houses were mostly of the small (usually three-bedroom) detached variety or semi-detached in the higher price bracket, some with four bedrooms and integral garage.[2]

Using figures adjusted to conform with the areas as they existed in 1931–39 the population of the Harrow UDC area grew from 49,020 in 1921 to 96,656 in 1931 and 190,200 in mid-1939; in the Ruislip-Northwood UDC area the growth through these years was 9,112, 16,035, 47,760; in Uxbridge UDC, 20,626, 31,887, 45,150; in Wembley MB it rose from 18,239 to 65,799 and then 121,600. At Rickmansworth the 1921 population of 8,634 had grown to 18,700 by mid-1938. Chorleywood's expansion was

[1] See the author's *London's Metropolitan Railway*, David & Charles, 1986, Chapter 15.

[2] Map 3 in The *Greater London Plan*, 1944, shows a respectable amount of 1918–39 private housing in the former Metro-land area to be of £1,000 value or above at 1940 prices.

much less spectacular and more widely dispersed, increasing from 2,444 in 1921 to 3,734 in mid-1938.

The number of ordinary tickets sold in March 1928 at all stations Wembley Park to Rickmansworth/Watford/Uxbridge inclusive was 164,834 (59 per cent) higher than the same figure for March 1923. Monthly season tickets issued at the same group of stations rose from 59,232 in March 1923 to 104,826 in March 1928, the steepest rises at Wembley Park to Pinner inclusive (up 33,984). In 1925 Metropolitan passenger earnings per Third Class seat were almost £67 compared with £64 on the Underground and £37 on the Southern Railway, the highest earner among the four big companies.

MRCE ordinary dividends rose from six per cent in the years 1926–29 to an 8 per cent peak in 1930 and 1931 before the economic depression knocked the figure back to 4 per cent in 1932 and 1933. On the Metropolitan Railway as a whole, the number of passenger journeys including season ticket holders increased from 87.8m in 1901 to 134.7m in 1930, the latter figure including the Great Northern & City Railway (20m in 1920).

As a device to promote traffic and direct choice of residential location to the railway's maximum benefit and as an object of publicity by the railway operators, Metro-land quickly faded into oblivion after 1933 but as may be deduced from the increase in Harrow's population between the wars shown above, the momentum for continued suburban growth in the area, notably on the south side of the Harrow–Uxbridge line, with cheaper housing, continued unchecked until the outbreak of World War 2 in September 1939. Calculations made by the LPTB in 1940 showed that between 1931 and 1939 the number of residents between West Harrow and Uxbridge rose from 48,300 to 95,000 (a 150 per cent increase). Between Preston Road and Harrow on the Hill, the growth was from 26,500 to 49,800; between Kingsbury and Stanmore from 17,800 to 33,100; and between North Harrow, Watford, Chesham and Amersham from 66,800 to 100,600. Most impressive of all the evidence of the phenomenal growth triggered off during 1930–37 were the figures issued to the Press by the LPTB in mid-1938 at the time of the rebuilding of two of the stations on the Uxbridge–Harrow line. These showed that the total number of passengers using Ruislip Manor station had increased from 17,000 in 1931 to 1,262,500 in 1937 and those at Rayners Lane from 22,000 in 1930 to four million in 1937.

After the formation of the LPTB on 1 July 1933, new building in what had been Metro-land continued unabated for almost seven years, most notably south of the line between West Harrow and Ruislip Manor stations. T F Nash Ltd used the railway to bring in building materials, seen here being transferred to their temporary narrow gauge light railway system at Rayners Lane goods yard. Nash's huge Tithe Farm Estate, not completed until the late 1930s, stretched almost to South Harrow. Others active in this area included Manor Homes (1932–9), Davis (1935–9), Crouch (1938–9) and Wimpey (1935–9).

After mid-1933, apart from Evelyn Waugh's fictional character, little more was heard of Metro-land until John Betjeman's poems of the 1950s and his BBC television programme of 1973.

Another more recent event makes a fitting conclusion for this account of London's Metro-land. The results of a 2004 study by the Department of Social Policy and Social Research at the University of Oxford must have wonderfully uplifted the spirits of Selbie, Wardle, 'F.', Sims, and Garland, wherever they abide, for it established that seventy-one years on, the happiest place in all England, that with the lowest levels of deprivation shown by the careful application of 37 different indices, was – *Chorleywood West*!

Appendices

APPENDIX 1:
RESIDENTIAL TRAIN SERVICES & TRAFFIC ON THE JOINT LINE IN THE EARLY 20th CENTURY

Photographs in the appendices were all taken in 2005.

When considering residential development within that part of Metro-land between Harrow and points beyond towards Aylesbury, it is important to bear in mind that from 1899 the Metropolitan's train services were supplemented by those of the Great Central Railway, which became part of the London & North Eastern Railway from 1 January 1923. This Appendix provides further detail and background on the section of 'shared' Metro-land between Harrow and Great Missenden/Chesham, particularly the outermost stations, which can be regarded as forming the limits of significant residential traffic.

With the opening of alternative access to London via Grendon Underwood, Ashendon Junction and Northolt Junction in 1906, some of the express services which had called at Aylesbury were diverted to the slightly longer but easier new route. At the same time the Metropolitan & Great Central Joint Committee was formed and the GCR began to operate outer suburban services over the Joint Line with new rolling stock. These were what contemporary writers were wont to call 'smartly-timed', particularly those at peak periods. By 1910 Harrow had 22 Down GCR trains and 24 Up on weekdays, the fastest timed at 13 minutes Down and 15 minutes Up. Pinner had 20 Down trains and 24 up, the fastest in 20/21 minutes. Northwood received 25 Down and 27 Up services including three Down and four Up, non stop rush hour journeys taking 21 minutes for the 13.75 miles. Chorley Wood was given 21 Down and 22 Up trains each weekday, some completing the 19½ miles with but one other stop in 32/33 min. The best of the 15 services each way at Amersham covered the 24 miles to and from Marylebone in 42/43 minutes, perhaps less impressive but all this offered serious competition for the Metropolitan and obviously played an important role in the development of 'shared' Metro-land. Yet the Metropolitan, with its Pullman car services (from 1910) and, above all, its through running to City stations probably had the edge. Marylebone was poorly sited for the major business districts of the capital, requiring a change to Underground or bus for the inner part of the commuter's journey.

Under the LNER regime, the Marylebone suburban services, by no means a main priority for the new management, became less attractive and, as mentioned in the main text, all regular LNER passenger trains were permanently withdrawn from the new branch to Watford after the start of the 1926 General Strike.

A detailed glimpse of the two companies' services in 'shared' Metro-land in 1912 was provided by the Rev. W J Scott in *The Railway & Travel Monthly* of January 1913. This account gives 37 minutes to Baker Street as the best time from Rickmansworth, described by Scott as 'a rather dull little town'. On weekdays, a total of 20 Metropolitan trains ran to London together with 24 GCR services (all to Marylebone). In the Down direction the respective totals were 21 and 25. For commuters, the Metropolitan provided Rickmansworth with four trains between 08.07 and 09.48, all running through to the City stations, whilst the GCR offered six departures for Marylebone between 07.41 and 09.31.

AT LITTLE CHALFONT

In some respects Chorley Wood, whose 'attractive position had made it a favourite residential centre' (Scott), did better. On weekdays, there were 41 Up trains and 37 Down, in business hours six GCR and five Metropolitan, all of the latter through to City stations. Up departures were timed to leave five (in one case six) minutes earlier than those just given from Rickmansworth. The best train took 38 minutes to reach Baker Street. Not only was there an additional train at 09.02; a call was also made by the last Up Pullman car train to the City, which did not stop at the 'rather dull little town' next door!

At Chalfont Road (now Chalfont & Latimer), the residential service was unimpressive, Scott remarking that more trains passed this station without stopping than any other between Rickmansworth and Aylesbury, 'nor does any really fast train of either partner call'. (The GCR's best time was 39 minutes for the 21¾ miles, an average of 33½ mph.) There were however about 18 trains a day shuttling to and from Chesham.

Chesham, 25¾ miles from Baker Street, enjoyed between 32 trains each way daily, including the branch shuttles. The journey to or from London usually took about an hour. Morning peak departures between 07.32 and 09.12 were provided by three GCR trains and two Metropolitan, all through to London, plus one shuttle branch train connecting with a Marylebone service at Chalfont Road.

Amersham had 28 trains each way daily to and from London, a total shared more or less equally by each company, including one 'fast' at 08.56 which reached Baker Street at 09.40 (36½ mph average speed).

Great Missenden was served by 28 Up trains and 30 Down, roughly shared equally by each company. One morning train from Marylebone passed Amersham but deigned to call here. The only 'fast' train started from Quainton Road at 08.08, calling at Great Missenden at 08.47, arriving at Baker Street at 09.40. This called at Wendover at 08.38.

Scott also provided details of the full 1912 Monday to Friday Pullman Car service, using information from W. Holt, the Metropolitan's Traffic Superintendent. This suggests the Pullman staff slept in the cars overnight and that maintenance and cleaning took place at Neasden. Reprovisioning was done at Liverpool Street.

Car *Galatea*:

Verney Jc depart 7.35 am (empty), Quainton Road depart 08.08 (empty), Aylesbury depart 8.26, semi-fast after Amersham, Baker St 9.40, Liverpool St 9.56 am, then empty to Neasden.

Empty from Neasden to Baker St, depart 12.05 pm, Willesden Green, Harrow and all stations to Aylesbury, arrive 1.34 pm, forms: 4.15 pm from Aylesbury, all stations to Harrow, Willesden Green, then Baker St, 5.46 pm, Liverpool St 6.01 pm.

Liverpool St depart 6.14 pm, Baker St 6.30 pm, non stop to Harrow, then all stations to Aylesbury 7.52 pm, Verney Jc 8.20 pm.

Verney Jc depart 9.15 pm, Aylesbury 9.47, most stations to Baker St arrive 11.17 pm.

Baker Street depart 11.35 pm, most stations to Aylesbury arrive 12.52 am.

Car *Mayflower*:

Aylesbury depart 6.24 am, Chesham depart 8.55, all stations to Harrow inclusive, Willesden Green, Baker St 9.50, Liverpool St 10.05 am.

Liverpool St depart 10.10 am, Baker St 10.26 am, Willesden Green, Harrow and stations to Aylesbury arrive 11.55 am.

Aylesbury depart 1.35 pm, passes Chalfont Road, Pinner and Northwood, Baker St 2.57 pm then to Neasden empty.

Neasden–Liverpool St empty arrive 5.18 pm.

Liverpool St depart 5.22 pm, Baker St 5.37 pm, Willesden Green and all stations from Harrow, Aylesbury arrive 7.01 pm.

The 1933 timetable[1] shows Rickmansworth benefiting from its new status as the outer terminus of Metropolitan electric services, with a prompt three-minute interchange between steam and electric traction for loco-hauled trains. This station had 49 trains a day each way (29 Met) with the fastest time to Baker Street now 26/27 minutes. Between 08.00 and 09.12 there were nine trains (four to Marylebone, fastest 26 min.). The 09.12 had a Pullman Car and like all the Met business trains, ran through to the City. Metropolitan season ticket revenue here in 1932 was £9,068.

There were 38 trains a day each way from Chorley Wood, 21 of them Metropolitan. Between 08.09 and 09.05, five Up trains left, including three for Marylebone, and the 09.05 took the Met Pullman car through to the City. During 1932, season ticket revenue here totalled £4,839, outstripping that for ordinary and workmen's tickets by almost £1,000.

[1] The information in these paragraphs is taken from the 1933 timetables, *Metro-land* 1932, 'Local Data' section, and Pick Box H 8 (London's Transport Museum)

Chalfont & Latimer was now almost equally busy, with a 1932 season ticket sale totalling £4,262, almost twice the other ticket receipts. Of the 39 trains a day each way, 22 were Metropolitan. There were five Up trains between 08.05 and the Pullman at 09.01, two of them to Marylebone.

Chesham's season ticket revenue in 1932 was £5,786, in this case almost £1,000 below other sales at this station. There were but 26 through services to and from London each way, 17 of them Metropolitan. Between 07.52 and the Pullman at 08.50 there were four trains, two to Marylebone; the best time to Baker Street was 51 minutes.

Amersham was now producing a season ticket revenue of £10,472, higher even than Rickmansworth and over £2300 more than other ticket income. Some of this commuter traffic would have originated from the MRCE's Weller Estate, contrary to earlier fears of a flop. There were 32 trains a day each way, 19 Metropolitan. The four rush hour departures for London between 07.47 and 08.57 (the Pullman) were equally shared by the Metropolitan and LNER, the former's best time to Baker Street being 40 min.

Great Missenden had 28 trains a day each way, 15 of them Metropolitan. Rush hour departures between 07.39 and the Pullman at 08.48 (Baker Street 09.39) totalled two for each partner. The season and other tickets here each yielded around £4,700.

At Wendover season ticket holders were thin on the ground, producing only around 23% of other ticket revenue; at Stoke Mandeville, commuters (many to Aylesbury?) contributed only £616, slightly less than other ticket receipts. Aylesbury's tickets brought in £13,387, of which seasons contributed only just over 16 per cent.

There were no season ticket holders at Waddesdon, Winslow Road or Verney Junction; the income from this source at Quainton Road was £77, at Granborough Road £14, and on the Brill Tramway £9.

AT CHORLEYWOOD

AT RICKMANSWORTH

AT WEMBLEY PARK

APPENDIX 2:
WEMBLEY PARK ESTATE 1915–1921

These summarised extracts are taken from Metropolitan Railway Board Reports, Board Minutes and Miscellaneous Papers. As the Metropolitan Railway Company was mortgagor of the Wembley Park Estate Company, all transactions on the Estate were reported to the Railway's Board; only a selection is shown here. Proceeds from sales were always retained by the Estate Company to enable it to continue to develop the Estate.

30.11.1915: 14 acres have been sold since building operations were started on the Estate Company's own account, the average price received is £785 an acre, sales have been mostly to individuals in single plots but 6.35 acres were sold to Messrs. Comben & Wakeling and 3.6 to Franklin and others. 185.36 acres are left unsold. The Estate Company have erected 26 houses at a cost of £420–£1,629 mostly in Oakington Avenue but also in Wembley Park Drive; of these 18 have been sold freehold, one leased for 99 years and of the balance all but one have been let. Eight more are being erected in Oakington Avenue at total cost of £3,360.

30.5.1918: All the houses erected by the Estate Company in Forty Lane and Oakington Avenue are now sold. 175.75 acres are still unsold. Recent sales have averaged £1,610 an acre for land.

18.9.1919: Various plots sold, average £1,508 an acre. 165.5 acres remain unsold.

13.11.1919: Various plots sold, average yield £764 an acre. 162.5 acres unsold. New road now being built on the Estate.

15.12.1919–3.1920: [Miscellaneous Papers MET 10/323]; Cyclops Construction Co. Ltd, lack of progress on contract with MRCE for construction of 40 houses at Neasden and 20 at Wembley Park owing to shortage of capital, difficulty in getting labour to travel out from London and difficulty in obtaining sand but Metropolitan Railway is now getting sand from Rickmansworth. In March 1920 Cyclops went into liquidation and were absorbed by MP Construction Ltd.

7.10.1920: Ten plots sold, £1,282 per acre average. 148.5 acres left.

26.5.1921: 18 plots sold, average £1,490 per acre, 145.25 acres left.

AT RAYNERS LANE

APPENDIX 3: ABERCROMBIE LOOKS UPON METRO-LAND, 1944

The Greater London Plan, 1944 by Professor Patrick Abercrombie MA, FRIBA, PPTPI, prepared on behalf of the Standing Conference on London Regional Planning at the request of the Minister of Town and Country Planning, was published in 1945 by His Majesty's Stationery Office. It contains some interesting comments on areas of Metro-land already experiencing railway-influenced residential development by 1933, growth which continued without effective planning control for a further six years. The text describes these places as they appeared to Abercrombie's team in the early 1940s after all house and amenity building had ceased owing to wartime restrictions. The relevant sections of the Abercrombie Report are: AMERSHAM & CHESHAM BOIS (309); CHALFONT ST GILES & CHALFONT ST PETER (311); CHORLEYWOOD* (344); MOOR PARK & BATCHWORTH (354); RICKMANSWORTH (357); WATFORD (364); ICKENHAM & HILLINGDON (380); UXBRIDGE (384).

Abercrombie did not hesitate to criticise the results of uncontrolled development up to 1940, giving detailed recommendations regarding prevention of further damage to sensitive environments. These proposals were often modified in practice, sometimes even completely ignored by the planning authorities. A few examples in what had been Metro-land follow.

CHESHAM BOIS, served by Amersham station (Amersham-on-the-Hill), was described as 'an expensive, almost suburban, residential area' having little community of interest with the old town of Chesham; there were few shops and it was 'hardly a town', despite coalescence with modern suburban development around Amersham station. A recommendation was made that separation should be be maintained between this area and old Amersham in the Misbourn Valley.

AT PINNER

Looking at the area around CHESHAM town, Abercombie deplored the modern development sprawling up the sides of the Chess and other valleys and also over the adjoining high land, recommending that expansion of the town should be rigidly limited.

CHORLEYWOOD[1] was seen as 'a purely residential sprawling low density dormitory suburb', largely dependent on the railway. The Report states that the small modern development near the station 'causes rather a harsh strident note as it climbs the hill-side nearby'. Abercrombie wanted no more building on the valley floor and no further outward expansion to be permitted anywhere.

Between RICKMANSWORTH and Chorleywood, Abercrombie wanted a 'broad belt of open country' to be maintained.

It is interesting to compare the information and proposals in the 1944 plan with the present situation as shown on contemporary maps and aerial photographs. This suggests significant growth has been allowed since, particularly around Amersham/Chesham Bois and Chorleywood/Rickmansworth, where developments begun in the Metro-land era and the six or so subsequent years have been subjected to new pressures and stimulation including the construction of the M25 motorway with convenient local access via Junction 18. Each station from Rickmansworth to Amersham inclusive now has its own considerable area of adjacent residential spread: Abercrombie's 'broad belt of open country' between Rickmansworth and Chorleywood is but a quarter-mile wide; less than a mile separates the latter from the built up area around Chalfont & Latimer station, a place now known as 'Little Chalfont' and a very narrow open strip offers little more than nominal separation between there and Amersham.

[1]*Charlewoode* was the ancient name, recorded as early as 1524. Distorted versions, *Charley Wood* or *Charleywood* remained in use in the 19th century, the former appearing on the 1822 Ordnance Survey map and the latter favoured as late as 1867 by the parish priest. The railway endorsed *Chorley Wood*, a form already in use, with the opening of its station in 1889 and this soon became generally acceptable, lasting until around the 1930s, when Chorleywood gained favour, a change belatedly accepted by the railway authorities in the early 1960s.

APPENDIX 4:
BEYOND AMERSHAM

As mentioned in Chapter 1, Metro-land's outermost boundaries never reached very far beyond Amersham in the Metropolitan Railway era but there were some interesting aspects to the outer section's traffic, which from 1899 had to be shared with the GCR and its successor, the LNER.

Following the arrival of the Metropolitan Railway in the area in the autumn of 1892, Lord Alfred Rothschild travelled to London from his country seat at Halton via the new Wendover station instead of using the LNWR at Tring. Fearing it might lose his patronage (worth some £600 a year at contemporary values) to the GCR, in 1895 the Metropolitan built two six-wheeled private saloons with accommodation for himself, his family and servants.

Another notable commuter was Sir Arthur Liberty, resident of Lee Manor, and founder of the famous Regent Street store, who had travelled up to London by horse coach, a journey of some 4½ hours. When the Metropolitan reached Great Missenden in 1892, he took the train on most weekdays. In the early 1900s he built a private road with locked gates to ease the journey to the station for his horses. However he appears to have transferred his custom to the GCR by that time, as he had a marble seat made and installed for his personal use at Marylebone should he arrive too early for his homebound train.

Upon the outbreak of war in August 1914, Rothschild gave his park and woodland to the Army as a training area. At first, the men were accommodated in tents but during the winter of 1914–15, wooden hutted camps were provided for the 20,000 troops who had arrived. In addition to the usual facilities, the camp had its own cinema and W. H. Smith bookstall and the Metropolitan Railway lost no time in announcing that its cheap fare tickets from central London were available for those 'desirous of witnessing the making of an Army'. Since Wendover booking office could not cope with the resulting traffic of troops, relatives, girlfriends and miscellaneous curious bystanders, a wooden temporary ticket office was erected on the platform in 1915.

In the summer of 1917 the site was taken over by the Royal Flying Corps (renamed the Royal Air Force from 1 April 1918) as a School of Technical Training, with German prisoners of war brought in to help with construction of the new facility. In 1918, at the suggestion of the Wendover stationmaster, the Germans built a 1.25-mile standard gauge light railway into the area from No.1 siding in Wendover freight yard. At its outer end, narrow gauge tracks were laid to facilitate the rebuilding and also to bring down timber from Rothschild's beech woods to be used for trench construction on the Western Front. Although most of the freight was handled by the GCR, the Metropolitan shared the boost to passenger traffic from this activity, this continuing on a smaller scale in peacetime, since Halton became a permanent RAF station and airfield. In the late 1920s, Willis H. Holt, the Metropolitan Traffic Superintendent, told Selbie in a paper about the allocation of steam locomotives that in connection with RAF leave arrangements and other requirements, as many as three special trains could be required at any one time at Wendover. Both the RAF station and its light railway outlasted the life of the Metropolitan. Latterly the railway carried mostly coal (up to 500 tons a week in winter) for the power station and heating.

Another special traffic also endured long after the disappearance of the Metropolitan. In 1917 Sir Arthur and Lady Lee presented their estate at Chequers, some 2½ miles south west of Wendover station, to be used as the official country seat of British Prime Ministers. For many years from 1921 this entailed rail travel to and from Wendover, not only by Prime Ministers from David Lloyd George onwards but by staff, guests and civil servants. An entry in the diary (*Whitehall Diary*) of Thomas Jones, Cabinet Secretary, for 26 April 1926 illustrates something of the routine at that time:

> We motored to Wendover. The PM bought the *Times*, *The Daily Telegraph*, *The Morning Post* and a picture paper for Mrs Baldwin ... He read the leading articles in less than five minutes, noticed the news of a friend's death and then settled down to solve a crossword puzzle in *The Daily Telegraph*, which he finished just as we steamed into Baker Street.' ['Steamed' is surely a slip of the pen!]

In the Metropolitan era, Stoke Mandeville was a quiet place, no more than a village,with a population of 356 in 1891 which had only grown to just over 600 by 1931. This station also served Weston Turville, east of the line, a duck breeding centre for many years and larger than its neighbour with almost 800 inhabitants in 1891. An article by W. E. Edwards in *The Railway Magazine* of October 1908 suggests there was a plan for the Metropolitan to move its works to Stoke Mandeville from Neasden and transfer of that site to the GCR, adding that a 'considerable extent of land' was acquired for this purpose. No mention of such a proposal appears in the Metropolitan Railway papers that survive other than a Board Minute of 21 December 1892 reporting that just over three acres adjoining the entrance to the booking office had been bought, no reason given. An area of that size would have accommodated only a small proportion of the then existing facilities at Neasden.

Excursion Traffic on the Aylesbury line 1920–22

When in June 1920 the Minister of Transport called upon the railways to resume excursion traffic, the Metropolitan agreed to run some half-day and full-day mid-week excursions from Aldgate to Aylesbury, calling at all stations from Rickmansworth inclusive. This sort of traffic was of course very sensitive to the weather; the highest number of tickets sold between 25 August and 30 September 1920 was 238 on 8 September, the lowest 34 on 16 September. The average over the period was 115, with Aylesbury, Wendover, Amersham, Chesham and Chorley Wood each featuring as the most popular destination on different days between 15 and 30 September. Similar excursions were operated in 1921 and 1922. The numbers travelling on Good Friday and Easter Monday in 1921 were respectively 461 and 1,267 (one train in duplicate), with Chorley Wood the most popular destination. For the same Easter days in 1922 the figures were 194 and 713 but on Whit Monday 1922, 1,493 excursion tickets were sold, the overflow being allowed on adjacent ordinary services. Again Chorley Wood was the most favoured destination, not the stations beyond.

APPENDIX 5: OUTER SECTION PASSENGER TRAFFIC & RECEIPTS, 1932

	Passenger Journeys	Passenger Receipts*
		£
GREAT MISSENDEN	63,580	10,412
WENDOVER	53,825	10,447
STOKE MANDEVILLE	16,891	1,089
AYLESBURY	131,480	30,431
WADDESDON	1,773	519
QUAINTON ROAD	10,598	601
GRANBOROUGH ROAD	2,237	124
WINSLOW ROAD	1,044	65
VERNEY JC	943	117
Brill Tramway		
BRILL & WOOD SIDING	3,272	191
WADDESDON ROAD	281	4
WESTCOTT	1,560	27
WOTTON	2,648	144

*Includes parcels and other items classified as passenger traffic

[From a paper prepared by George Hally (former Traffic Manager, Metropolitan Rly) for an inspection visit by Frank Pick and other LPTB officers and officials and LNER officers and officials to the Metropolitan & GC Joint Line stations on 1 August 1933 (Pick file H 8, London's Transport Museum)]

SOURCES

The extensive series of Metropolitan Railway papers in the London Metropolitan Archives under the general classification ACC 1297. Also Pick File H8, London's Transport Museum.

The collection of Metropolitan Railway publicity and related ephemera held by London's Transport Museum, notably copies of various editions of *Metro-land* also other copies of that publication and miscellaneous Metropolitan railway ephemera held in the private collections of Trevor Wayman, Mike Miller, Graham Page and the author.

Reference was also made to some of the items listed in the Select Bibliography opposite.

SELECT BIBLIOGRAPHY

Abercrombie, Patrick, *Greater London Plan 1944*, His Majesty's Stationery Office 1945

Anon, Brochures for plot sales on The Headstone Estate, Harrow-on-the-Hill (with plans) 8.7.1899 (83 plots), 23.9.1899 (89 plots); 3.4.1901 (50 plots); 22.6.1901 (60 plots), Clarke & Charles, Harrow

Anon, Prospectus, Ruislip Manor Ltd, 19 December 1910

Anon, Brochure, Ruislip Manor Cottage Society Ltd, including description of the development scheme, with plans of Houses and full particulars, 1912

Anon, First Edition *The Moor Park Estate in the Counties of Hertford and Middlesex. Illustrated Particulars, Plan and Conditions of Sale*, Knight, Frank & Rutley, 1919

Anon, *Moor Park Limited, Views and Plans of the Club House, Golf Courses, Park and Estate*, Moor Park Ltd, 1922

Anon. *The Authentic Map Directory of London and Suburbs*, First Edition, Geographia (1923) Ltd, 1924

Anon, *Cassiobury Park Estate*, Cassiobury Park Estates Ltd, 1930 (?)

Anon, *T F Nash Builders South Harrow & Rayners Lane*, Brochure, 1933

Bain, James, *The Authentic Map Directory of London and Suburbs,* Third Edition, Geographia Ltd, 1933

Bowlt, Eileen M, *The Goodliest Place in Middlesex* [Ruislip], Hillingdon Borough Libraries, 1989

Cooper, Elizabeth (Editor), *Harrow Miscellany,* Harrow WEA Local History Group, 1975

Cooper, Elizabeth, *Pinner Streets Yesterday and Today*, Pinner & Hatch End Local Historical & Archaeological Society, 1976

Dark, Arthur, *From Rural Middlesex to London Borough: The Growth and Development of Harrow Illustrated with Maps*, London Borough of Harrow, 1981

Edwards, Dennis, *London's Underground Suburbs*, Capital Transport Publishing, Second Edition, 2003

Edwards, Ron, *Eastcote From Village to Suburb,* Hillingdon Borough Libraries, 1987

Green, Frank & Wolff, Dr Sidney F., *London and Suburbs Old and New*, Souvenir Magazines Ltd, 1933

Head, Barry, *The Northwood Book* Vol. II, Author, 1984

Hewlett, Geoffrey, (Editor), *A History of Wembley*, Brent Library Service, 1979

Jackson, Alan A, *London's Metropolitan Railway*, David & Charles, 1986

Jackson, Alan A, *Semi-Detached London*, Wild Swan, Second Edition, 1991

Johnson, Stuart, (Editor) *Queensbury: A Short History*, Wembley History Society, 1986

Row, Prescott & Anderson, Henry, (Editors). *Where to Live Round London (Northern Side)*, Homeland Association Ltd, Third and Revised Edition, 1910–11

Stanford, William, *Bacon's Large Scale Atlas of London and Suburbs*, G. W. Bacon & Co. Ltd, editions 1904, 1912, 1928

Tottman, David, *Ruislip-Northwood: An Early Example of Town Planning and its Consequences*, Ruislip, Northwood & Eastcote Local History Society, Occasional Paper No. 2, 1982

Valentine, K J, *Neasden: A Historical Study,* Charles Skilton, 1989

Ordnance Survey Maps 6 in to 1 mile, various editions; 1 in to 1 mile, The Chilterns 1931; Seventh Series, Sheet 159 *The Chilterns* 1950–56; Seventh Series, Sheet 160 *London N W* 1958.

Newspapers & Magazines *Evening News* London, 1901–1940 (advertisements), *Estates Gazette*, *The Railway Magazine*, *Railway & Travel Monthly*.

MY LITTLE METRO-LAND HOME.

VOCAL ONE-STEP.

Words by
BOYLE LAWRENCE.

Music by
HENRY THRAILE.

H.D.M.P.C[o] 944.

I She smiles as I run Down the cool shad-y lane, The
day has be-gun In the eight-fif-teen train.
rall.
REFRAIN.
There's a lit-tle wife, The joy of my life In a trim lit-tle bung-ga-
p-f
low. There's a lit-tle dot In a lit-tle cot

3

In a lit - tle spot
A lit - tle spot that I know; To the hum of
bees, And whis - per of trees At twi-light to - geth - er we
roam. It's hap-pi-ness crowned, It is Pa-ra-dise found Is
my lit - tle Met-ro-land home.
home.
1.
2.
f
fz
H.D.M.P.Cº 944.

Till ready.
A smile sweet and rare, And a wel-come so
gay Are wait-ing me there At the close of the day. Each
eve'-ning at sev'n She is look-ing for me When I
get back to Heav'n By the five fif-ty three.
mf
p
rall.

H. D. M. P. C^{o} 944.

REFRAIN.
There's a lit - tle wife, The joy of my life
In a trim lit - tle bun - ga - low.
There's a lit - tle dot In a lit - tle cot
In a lit - tle spot A lit - tle spot that I know;
H. D. M. P. Co. 944.

To the hum of bees, And whisper of trees At
twi-light to-geth-er we roam. It's hap-pi-ness crowned,
It is Pa-ra-dise found Is my lit-tle Met-ro-land
1.
home.
2.
home.
f
fz
H.D.M.P.Cº 944

Straight on to "Trio" when the number is used as a Dance.

H.D.M.P. Cº 944. The Era Press, Leyton. E.10.

Index

NOTE There may be more than one reference on the page indicated.
Figures in bold type indicate illustrations, maps and plans; there is often also a reference in the text on the page shown.